CHAOS TO HARMONY

A different way to face life's challenges, build resilience, and live the life you want

by Andres Ponciano

Chaos to harmony: A different way to face life's challenges, build resilience, and live the life you want

Copyright © 2018 by Andres Ponciano. All Rights Reserved.

All rights reserved. No part of this book may be reproduced in any form or by any electronic or mechanical means including information storage and retrieval systems, without permission in writing from the author. The only exception is by a reviewer, who may quote short excerpts in a review.

Cover design by Reychelle Ann Ignacio of
Marketplace Designers

All illustrations by Andres Ponciano
unless otherwise stated

Visit my website at www.bigskill.org

Printed in the United States of America

ISBN Paperback: 9781718007147

Visit our website and join our newsletter

If you'd like to read more interesting content, please visit our website at: **https://bigskill.org**

You can also join our weekly email newsletter to receive updates and new articles by going here: **http://eepurl.com/dCkkZb**

*To my nephews, Dominic and Lucas.
Whatever path you take, I hope this book encourages,
guides, and provides some truth along the way.*

Table of contents

INTRODUCTION	8
PART 1 - Choose who you want to be, the life you want, and get to work	16
Spending time in solitude	17
Experiment and test, test, test	21
Make the decision	23
Purpose, Action, Motivation	28
End vs. Process	31
Prepare	34
Seeing the future\ Anticipating	37
The value of curiosity	40
List your models	45
Mindfulness and breathing	47
Taking immediate action	50
Discipline, consistency, and focus	54
Go Pro	61
Love the work	63
The process is the way	66
Constant growth	69
Challenge, ability, and flow	72
PART 2 - THE WHEEL OF EMOTIONS	75
Figuring out your emotions so you can move forward	76
PART 3- PUTTING LIFE'S CHALLENGES IN PERSPECTIVE	81
PARADOX	82
Yin and Yang	83
Pain, suffering, and joy	84
Happiness and sadness	88
Fear and courage	90
CONTEXT	94
How it all makes sense	95
The details, bigger picture, going deep, and applying wide	98
Re-framing perspectives	102
Three different meanings	106

Zimbardo's time perspectives	108
Long term vs. Short term thinking	112
Cycles	117
The art of proving yourself wrong	122

Part 4 - STRATEGIES TO COPE WITH LIFE'S CHALLENGES AND BUILD RESILIENCE — 126

Deconstruct Things	127
Self talk	133
Optimism	136
Frustration + Curiosity = Progress	139
Solution focused thinking leads to possibilities	142
Accountability	146
Not taking it personally	149
Feedback & measuring progress	151
Compete	155
Be okay looking foolish	157
What would 'they' do?	159
Gratitude and enthusiasm	161
What you've overcome	166
Find the humor, laugh, have fun, and play	167
Pushing out of your comfort zone	171
Don't stop pushing yet	175
Getting used to stress	177
Limiting Factors	182
Emotional control	187
Rejection	191
Embracing failure	195
The Stoic Philosophy	200
Insecurity & Uncertainty	204
Attachment & Detachment	208
Patience	212
Hard choices	215
The relationships you build	217

PART 5 - Implementing the ideas — 222

Deliberate Practice	223

How to practice	225
Sample Ideas	226
Conclusion	**230**
SHARE & REVIEW	**231**
List of people to study	**232**

INTRODUCTION

What will cause you the most suffering in life?

> *"We are threatened with suffering from three directions: from our own body, which is doomed to decay and dissolution and which cannot even do without pain and anxiety as warning signals; from the external world, which may rage against us with overwhelming and merciless forces of destruction; and finally from our relations to other men. The suffering which comes from this last source is perhaps more painful to us than any other."*
>
> - Sigmund Freud[1]

Freud believed the decay of our body, Mother Nature, and other people are the "three directions" that cause us most suffering. The problem is that we can't do much about any of these things. We can't control Mother Nature, much less other people. We can try to take as much care of our body, but time will wear it down either way. Suffering comes from the way we perceive how these events affect our life. How we choose to view them is within our control. The "direction" which will cause us the most suffering, then, is ourselves.

---

[1] Freud, Sigmund, and James Strachey. *Civilization and Its Discontents*. New York: W.W. Norton & Company, 2010. Print.

If you can't face the challenges life throws at you and appreciate how you can grow from them, you'll continue suffering. You'll never be the person you could be. You'll never live the life you want.

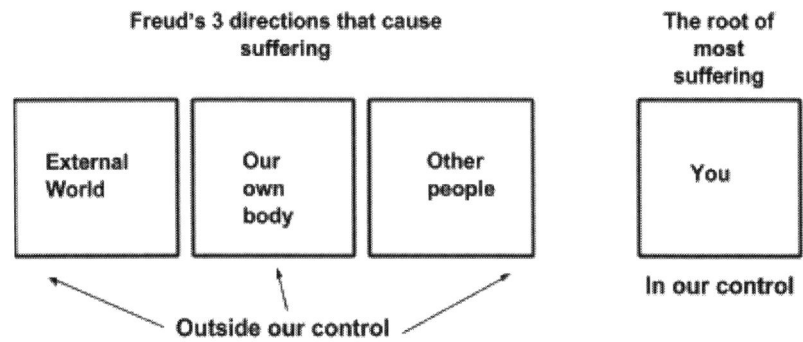

Resistance

"Most of us have two lives: the life we live, and the unlived life within us. Between the two stands Resistance."

-Steven Pressfield

In order to become the person we want to be, we have to overcome the resistance. That means doing things we've never done. It means stepping out of our comfort zone and feeling uncomfortable. It means constantly challenging and pushing ourselves to go to the next level.

Try drawing or writing out a description of who you are today, at this moment.

Now do the same thing for the person you want to be.

Then answer these questions:

- Why do you want to be that person?
- What difficult things do you need to do to get there and how will doing them get you there?
- Who can help you get there?
- Where is the best place to be to increase the probability of getting there?
- When do you plan to get there?

Now, set a deadline to meet the future you, face to face.

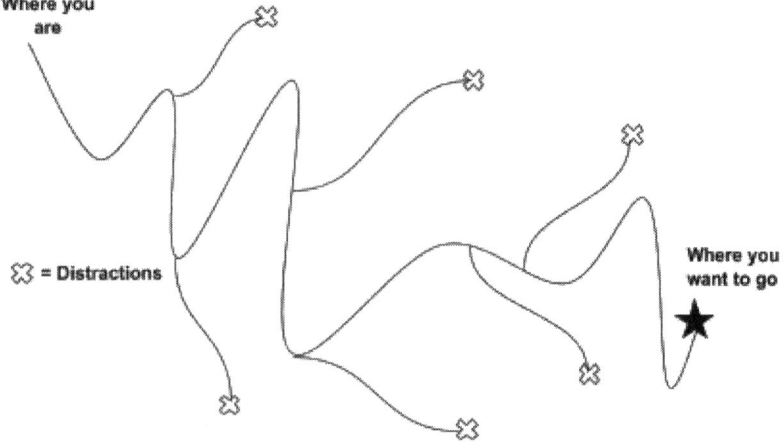

Going through resistance

A guitar player develops calluses on the tips of his fingers when starting to play the guitar. This initial period is painful. Many beginners give up at this point. They can't handle the pain. They aren't willing to wait for the calluses on their fingertips to harden, so they can move on to playing and making music. We make the choice to let the pain of playing guitar in the beginning, be greater than the pleasure of making music.

Life forces us to stretch, whether we choose to or not. We either break down or we grow stronger and more resistant as a result. When we stretch and push past our limits, we build calluses in our body and our mind.

The people that go through resistance view adversity in a way that allows them to move past any obstacles, grow stronger, and get what they want out of life.

The purpose of this book is to help you build that mindset. In doing this, you'll be able to take advantage of the opportunities you encounter on your path and enjoy the many pleasures, which pain brings.

> "Never forget: This very moment, we can change our lives. There never was a moment, and never will be, when we are without the power to alter our destiny. This second, we can turn the tables on Resistance. This second, we can sit down and do our work."
> —**Steven Pressfield**

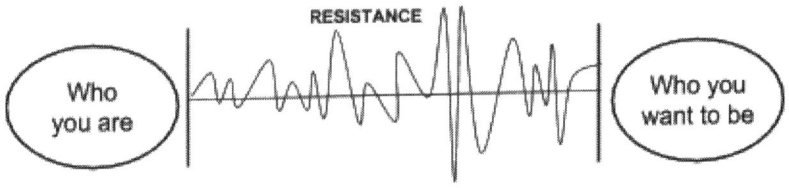

Keep this in mind

What is shared here is what works for me. That doesn't mean it'll work for you. You can read Einstein's biography, put all his lessons and ideas to work, but that doesn't mean you'll be the next Einstein. There are characteristics that are unique to him, which you may or may not possess. Do you have Einstein's work ethic, his power to focus on one thing for extended periods of time, his mindset of constant questioning, his patience, his vision, and imagination?

That is why you often read this:

***Results may vary.

The ideas presented here have different perspectives. You would benefit in testing those out as well. There is something to learn from them.

The question is not what is right and what is wrong, but "in this particular situation, at this moment, what is going to work and what is not?" Each situation is unique. It's not a one-size fits all approach. What worked well one moment, won't necessarily work well in another.

Keep an open mind and play around with these ideas. Hopefully, you'll find some that work for you.

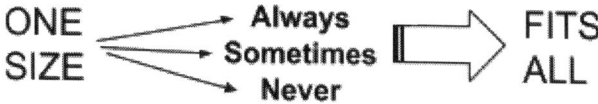

The book is divided into 5 different parts

Part 1- This focuses on you; where you want to go and your purpose for wanting it. It'll ask questions to determine what needs to be done to get to where and who you want to be. It also provides useful ideas to best prepare for the long road ahead.

Part 2- This part requires reflection and paying attention to what you're feeling as you go through the process of getting to where you want.

Part 3- You'll find a variety of different ways to view challenges. This section will help put things in perspective.

Part 4- Discusses different concepts to cope with life's challenges and help you build resilience. It provides questions and exercises to get you thinking, questioning, and applying the ideas. The questions are designed to get you out of your usual thinking and open the door to other possibilities. They are a valuable part of the process. You may already be familiar with some of the ideas and applications, while others will be new. Feel free to jump around to different sections of this part based on what is important to you.

Part 5 - This part will help implement the ideas in the book and provide you sample ways to practice the concepts.

At the end, you'll find a list of books, interviews, and documents that were used to research and write this book. You can use it to dive further into each topic.

PART 1 - Choose who you want to be, the life you want, and get to work

Spending time in solitude

> "Solitude is painful when one is young,
> but delightful when one is more mature."
>
> - Albert Einstein

Humans are social beings.

Lieberman in his book, 'Social,' says, "*Food, water, and shelter are not the most basic needs for an infant. Instead, being socially connected and cared for is paramount. Without social support, infants will never survive to become adults who can provide for themselves. Being socially connected is a need with a capital N.*" [2]

Without the social connection to caretakers, infants would be helpless and they'd die. In the past, an adult thrown out of their tribe wouldn't have access to the food, shelter, and protection of the group. This was a death sentence.

It explains why people who are loners or spend lots of time on their own, are often seen as strange or anti-social. Yet, solitude provides many benefits that are hard to come by when we are constantly distracted, by the company of others.

---

[2] Lieberman, Matthew D. *Social : why our brains are wired to connect.* New York: Crown Publishers, 2013. Print.

Sara Maitland in, *How to be alone,*[3] discusses how different groups of people encourage spending time alone. The Aborigines, for example, sent their kids on a six month "walkabout," in order to prepare them for adulthood. Monks and knights spent time alone prior to their initiation and called it a "vigil."

Today, some Ivy League universities encourage gap years. A year after high school and before university where students do volunteer work, travel, try different jobs, and experience the world on their own. This helps them gain independence, get to know themselves, and experience life in different ways. It also helps them determine what they want to do with their life. That way, they'll be more certain of what they choose to study in university and increase the probability of it being fulfilling and rewarding.

Many artists and creative people seek spaces where they can work without distractions. This leads them to long periods of time in solitude. But this solitude also allows them to fully focus and develop their creativity. Henry David Thoreau wrote his famous book, *Walden*, while spending two years alone at Walden Pond. Spending time on your own is a way to bring out your creativity and produce great work.

Solitude forces you to spend time with yourself; getting to know who you are, what you think, why you think that way, your dreams and fears, what you're good at, what you're not. It helps

---

[3] Maitland, Sara. *How to be alone*. London: Macmillan, 2014. Print.

you understand what you want out of life and where you're at, this very moment. It allows you to reflect and get a clear picture.

Getting to know yourself is not a destination. You're a living, breathing thing, and you're constantly changing. What you once considered important and what you wanted when you were young, is likely to change. Continue getting to know yourself by experimenting and reflecting. You may never know everything about yourself. The more layers you peel back, the more interesting your path to discovery.

How you get to know yourself

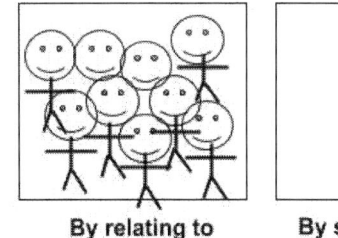
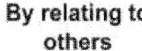

By relating to others   By spending time alone   By trying many things

Some ideas to embrace solitude:

- Go into nature. Go for walks, ride a bike, paddle a boat, ride a hot air balloon.
- Be fully present. Be mindful.
- Plan out alone time. Go on your own adventures to new places.
- Travel alone.
- Do activities on your own. Go to the movies, a cafe, a museum.

- Reflect daily on your life.
- Ask yourself questions.
- Get to know yourself by experimenting.
- Create something on your own.

Experiment and test, test, test

"Everybody's a mad scientist, and life is their lab. We're all trying to experiment to find a way to live, to solve problems, to fend off madness and chaos.

-David Cronenberg

Be like a scientist, constantly asking questions, then making hypotheses and experimenting, observing what occurs, coming to conclusions and then testing again. Each time leading to new questions. We have to be able to test, test, and test. There is more than one approach and there is one that would be better suited for us, at this moment. In order to find what works best, you have to test constantly and adjust.

When you write an essay in school you start by writing a rough draft. The teacher corrects it, provides feedback, and you then write another draft. The teacher goes through it again, provides more feedback, and then you write the final draft.

But what if we were to write 5 rough drafts before ever handing one in? What would the first rough draft the teacher receives, look like?

In marketing you have to constantly be testing a variety of things. An advertisement, for example; what you think is going to get people to respond the most, is often not the best choice. You only know what works well by testing; testing the copy, the colors, and the design.

By doing this, you will learn something new.

Things to try:

- Create experiments and write down what you expect to happen and other possibilities.
- Observe as you put it to the test and take note of what happens.
- Did what you expect to happen occur? If not, why?
- What did you learn?
- How can you adjust it to get your desired outcome?
- Now try again.
- Create many drafts before getting to the final draft. Keep in mind that the final draft can still be improved.

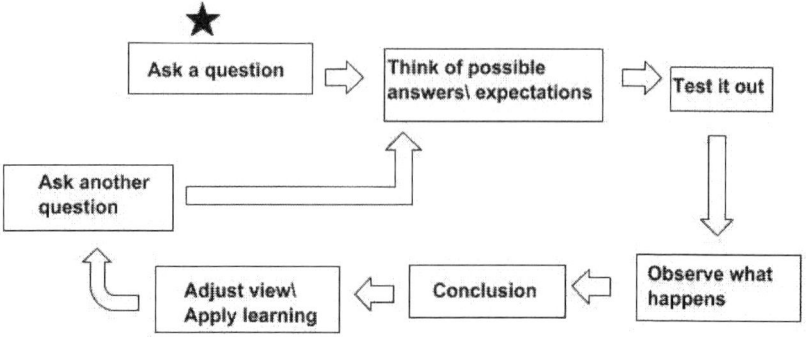

Make the decision

"It is hard to imagine a more stupid or more dangerous way of making decisions than by putting those decisions in the hands of people who pay no price for being wrong."

-Thomas Sowell

What you want is waiting for you. You have to decide to go and get it. It's easier to make a decision when we're clear on our purpose. It may be as simple as asking whether this decision is taking me closer or further from what I want.

Other times, it's not as simple.

Decide what you want. If you change your mind along the way, that's fine. Making the choice to go one direction, beats waiting for the right moment, the right circumstances, or more information, to make the right decision.

The one who wins, is the one that can take any circumstances they are dealt and still play a great game.

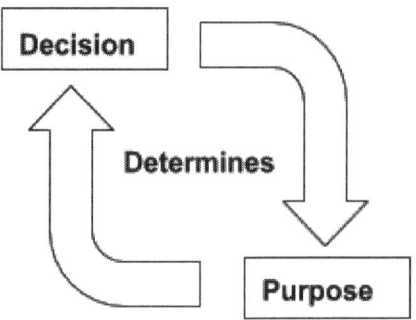

Here are some reasons we make bad decisions:

- We don't have experience to draw from in the situation.
- We have an immediate pay off that is positive and overlook the long term effects which are negative.
- We don't consider the consequences of what we decide.
- We don't know ourselves well enough. We don't know our strengths, weaknesses, we have no clear purpose.
- We are blind to our own biases and have few tools to approach different problems.
- We don't consider different options.
- We don't understand certainty, uncertainty, risk, reward, opportunity cost, and probability.

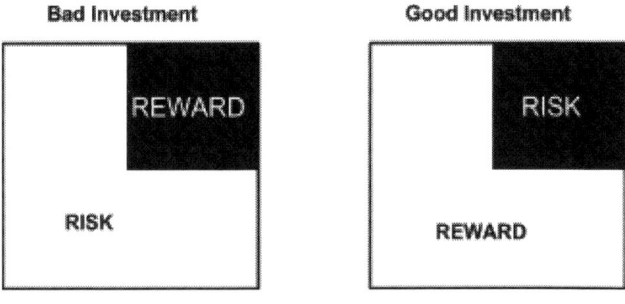

Here is what we can do about the above:

- Study and learn from history about what works and what doesn't. Read biographies of people who have gone through similar situations or who have achieved what you want and learn how they did it. Deconstruct people into strong skills they possess. Work on developing those skills. Stay curious and constantly search for ideas.

- Consider the longer term consequences by asking *"and then what"* would happen if I did this? Do it a few times. Look for the potential problem areas beforehand.

- Get to know yourself. Experiment a variety of things in life, in work, in relationships, in different environments. Travel. Then reflect on what you've learned about yourself through those situations.

- Ask for feedback and different opinions from a variety of people to get more perspective.

- Learn different ways to solve problems. Search for ideas.

- Consider all the options you have and rate them.

- Consider the certainty, uncertainty, risk, reward, opportunity cost, and probability in your possible choices.

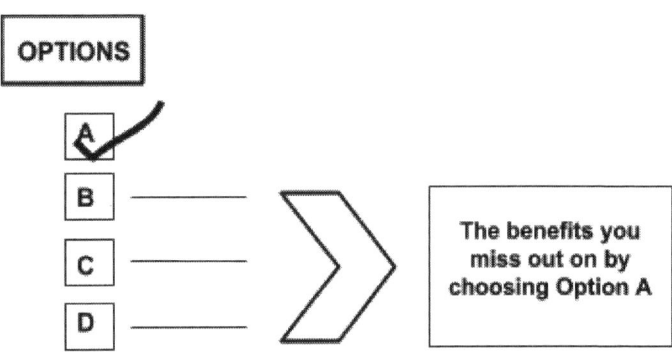

In, *Take the Risk*,[4] Dr. Ben Carson discusses four simple questions to ask yourself in order to make a decision. They are:

- What is the best that can happen if you do this?
- What is the best that can happen if you don't do this?
- What is the worst that can happen if you do this?
- What is the worst that can happen if you don't do this?

These questions provide a simple way to uncover and assess the pros and cons of your options.

QUESTIONS

- What are the different outcomes and their probability of occurring?
- What is the opportunity cost? The tradeoff you are making?

---

[4] Carson, Ben, and Gregg Lewis. *Take the risk : learning to identify, choose, and live with acceptable risk*. Grand Rapids, Mich: Zondervan, 2008. Print.

- What is the best\ worst that can happen if I do it or if I don't do it?
- What are some of the most difficult decisions I've had to make and how did I do it? What was the result of those decisions?
- How can I improve the chance of being right in my choices?
- What other tools can I use to make good decisions?
- Am I being biased and is that affecting my ability to see clearly?
- Who can provide good advice or help?

What you know ●

What you think you know

All the white space is what you don't know!

Purpose, Action, Motivation

David Goggins, an ex-Navy SEAL, believes purpose is more powerful than motivation. Motivation comes and goes. A purpose will drive you forward and allow you to overcome obstacles.

In an interview,[5] Goggins talks about how he signed up for a trial run so he could participate in the ultramarathon, Badwater 135. To qualify for the race he had to run 100 laps around a 1 mile track. That's a total of 100 miles and he had to do it in 24 hours or less. He was participating in order to raise money for the Special Operations Warrior Foundation. An organization that provides full tuition scholarships to children of military families. Even though he hadn't trained for the race at all, was out of shape, and hated running, Goggins went for it.

He ran 70 miles and had to take a break. Goggins had shin splints, stress fractures and couldn't even get up to go to the bathroom. He had placed tape around his feet, ankles and shins to help support his weight as he ran. His wife told him he wouldn't be able to run the remaining laps. Motivated by what she said and driven by his purpose, Goggins pushed through anyway. The purpose he had for doing this was more important than the pain he felt. The purpose created the motivation to take necessary action.

A clear purpose will have the same effect for you.

---

[5] Bilyeu, Tom. "How to Make Yourself Immune to Pain | David Goggins on Impact Theory." *YouTube*, 23 May 2017, www.youtube.com/watch?v=78I9dTB9vqM.

Sometimes we get hung up trying to think of what our purpose is. We forget that even after making a decision, we can still change it. If you decide on something that doesn't work for you, you are smart enough to realize it and can then adjust. You just need to pay attention.

William Faulkner said, *"I only write when I'm inspired. Fortunately I'm inspired at 9 o'clock every morning."* His inspiration came from having the discipline to sit down and write. Every. Single. Day.

Charlie Banacos, a legendary music and improvisation teacher I was fortunate to study with, once told me that, *"motivation was overvalued. Motivation came easily once you got momentum. To create momentum, you just had to start."* That is often the hardest part. Getting started. Once you start, it's much easier to keep going.

Freud said, *"Just as a cautious businessman avoids tying up all his capital in one concern, so, perhaps, worldly wisdom will advise us not to look for the whole of our satisfaction from a single aspiration."*

It is better to have a big list of things that bring you satisfaction in life. That way, when you lose one, the rest make up for it. Similarly, it is better to have many reasons for doing something. That way, if one reason changes or becomes unimportant, you'll have others to keep you going and taking action.

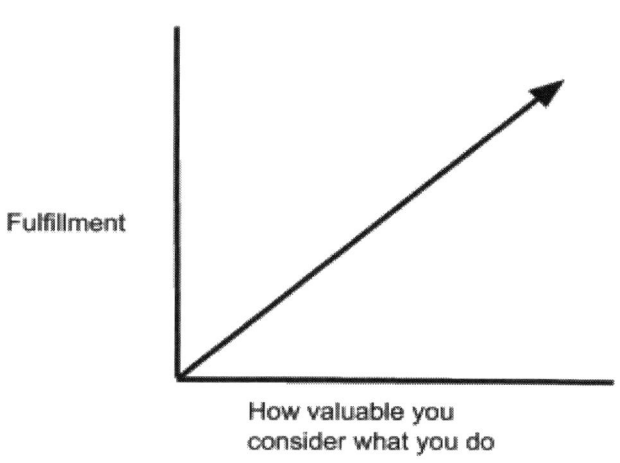

QUESTIONS

- Why do you do what you do? What is your purpose in doing this? Is there only one? Can you think of more?
- What excites you most about this?
- What worries\ scares you the most?
- What are the things that bring you satisfaction?
- How do they satisfy you?
- What are the things you value most?

End vs. Process

Once you know where you want to go and why you want to go there, you're going to need a road map. The end result you desire is where you're headed. Think of how long it will take to get there.

Break it down.

Ask yourself the following questions:

- What needs to be done each month in order to achieve the end result?
- What needs to be done each week?
- What about each day? Each hour?

Focus on carrying out the daily process. Then track your progress daily.

Example: Write a 150,000 word novel in 6 months.

- Month 1 = Research, create an outline, think of story and characters.
- Month 2 - - - > Month 5 = Write at least 37,500 words every month.
- Month 6 = Edit, revise and publish.

Now, break down each month into weekly tasks.

- Month 1, Week 1 = Think of a story and interesting characters. What are the motivations of the characters? What's the point of the story? Read books and get inspired. List ideas of interesting things.

- Month 1, Week 2 = Keep reading books and getting inspired. Start researching specific topics you want to write about in the book. Create a description of the characters and start working on the outline.

- Month 1, Week 3 to Week 4 = Keep researching, developing characters, and working on the outline.

- Month 2, Week 1 ---> Month 5, Week 4 = Using your outline and all your research, begin writing. Write a minimum of 8,750 words each week.

- Month 6, Week 1 ---> Week 4 = Edit, revise and publish.

Break down each week into daily tasks. (For simplicity's sake, we'll look at only one section.)

- Month 2 ---> Month 5 = Write a minimum of 1,250 words every day.

Break it down into hourly tasks:

- Month 2 ---> Month 5 = Write from 6AM to 8AM, every day. Write a minimum of 625 words per hour.

Once this is clear, focus on the hourly tasks. Assess progress and how well you keep to your plan, every day. Don't focus on the end result. Focus on every hour.

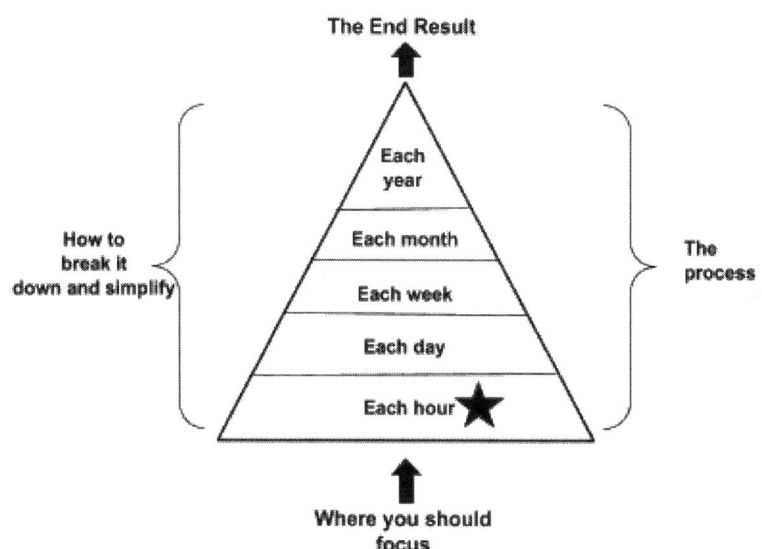

Prepare

> *"Be prepared, work hard, and hope for a little luck. Recognize that the harder you work and the better prepared you are, the more luck you might have."*
>
> -Ed Bradley

The best way to deal with any challenges is to be prepared for them. You can't prepare for everything in life. There are always going to be unknowns. You could set everything up perfectly, but then something occurs, that changes everything.

There are always surprises, but the more prepared you are, the better you'll handle the situations that come out of nowhere.

Here are some things that will challenge us and those close to us:

- The death of a loved one
- The loss of a job
- Not being able to live off what you love or hating your job
- Not getting what you want
- Seeing life pass you by, still doing the same thing, and being unhappy
- Going through pain and difficulty to achieve what you want

- Realizing your dreams may be unattainable or very difficult to achieve
- Losing control of your body, paralysis
- Having an addiction you can no longer control
- The ending of a relationship, seeing your parents separate
- Finding out you have a disease, knowing there is no cure for it
- Finding out you're not very good at what you think you're good at
- Losing your home and ending up homeless
- Being broke
- Having no friends
- Not being wanted or loved by your parents
- Being in an accident and not being physically able to do what you used to
- Waving off a loved one because they're going to fight a war, being in a war you don't want to be in
- Losing every possession you have
- Losing family, friends and having to leave your country to find a safe place to live
- Being held at gunpoint
- Getting on a raft to seek refuge in another country
- Risking your life to have more opportunity and help your family
- Being a victim of physical, verbal or sexual abuse
- An unexpected pregnancy, a kidnapping
- Not liking yourself
- Closing down your business and having to let everyone go
- Being unemployed and having a family to take care of
- Firing people

Things to try:

- In every area of your life, think of three outcomes. The best case scenario, the worst case scenario, and the most likely scenario. What will you do in each case?
- Consider some of the above scenarios and how you would respond to them.
- Think of the negative parts of each situation. Are there any positives?
- Think of how many of these you've had to go through or haven't gone through. What about people you know?

Then remember this:

"No matter how good you have it, there is someone that has it better. No matter how bad you have it, there is someone that has it worse."

Be grateful for the life you have.

Seeing the future\ Anticipating

"Anticipate the difficult by managing the easy."

-Lao Zi

Peak into the future. Think of who you want to be and what you want in your life. Then think about all the things that can go wrong. The setbacks you'll encounter, the obstacles along the way, the failure. Now consider all the ways you can overcome these challenges. Prepare for them beforehand, so that when they come, (and they will), you are better suited to face them.

Have an idea of the person you want to be. Have an idea of the person you definitely don't want to be. Think about how your life will look, how you will act, the people in your life, how others will treat you, and how you'll perceive difficulties. Think about the things that will allow you to get there. What kinds of skills and habits do you have to develop?

Work on that daily.

Pre-mortems

When a company goes out of business it's common to do a post mortem. The investors or owners review the reasons why the company failed, what went wrong, and what can be learned from the situation. It's also something people do after relationships end. But what if you did the opposite?

Many startups use this idea to determine where things can go wrong, where mistakes are likely to happen, and how they can best position themselves for success.

A pre-mortem asks you to think one year into the future after your business has failed. What were the reasons for the failure? Take those reasons and have solutions for every one of them. You prepare beforehand, by making sure you don't allow those issues to cause damage to your business from the start. You are better positioned for success by taking pre-emptive action. This concept can be applied to all areas of your life.

Things to try:

- In a relationship, your job, your health, think of everything that could go wrong. Do a pre-mortem and come up with ways to prepare for these situations or prevent them from occurring.

{ What won't change

  What might change

  The many unknowns }   **Prepare and anticipate different scenarios**

The value of curiosity

"The important thing is not to stop questioning. Curiosity has its own reason for existing."

– Albert Einstein

Our desire to know makes us curious and this leads us to ask questions, look for answers, and move forward. Questions create more questions and it becomes a never ending cycle of discovery.

Curiosity helps us to gather knowledge. The more we gather, the better prepared we are to adjust to changing circumstances. We can't adapt, if we don't know what we're adapting to.

If you've ever asked why something is the way it is, how things work or what this means, that is your curiosity at work. The space between knowing something and not knowing, forms the curiosity gap. Humans have a built in desire to fill this gap.

By asking questions, we come to understand ourselves and other people. We see a clearer picture of what is around us. Questions lead to better thinking. Many times we fear questioning. In school, we worry the other kids will laugh at us. Teachers sometimes discourage questions and we end up accepting and not questioning what they say. Let go of the fear of being laughed at and called a fool. Question your teachers, your parents, your friends, everyone you meet. Do it from a place of wanting to learn. The more curious you become, the less bored you'll be. Curious people keep themselves busy; wanting to know more about the world around them. This is what drives progress in all fields.

According to Ian Leslie in his book, *Curious*,[6] there are two kinds of curiosity; diversive and epistemic.

Diversive is the kind of curiosity that seeks excitement and novelty. It's what keeps you scrolling through your social media feed non-stop into the night. You're looking for anything entertaining. Epistemic curiosity seeks to go deeper into an area to learn something new. You see an interesting article, you read it, then search more on the topic, and go deeper. Learn to use both types to your benefit.

As we age, we lose our curiosity. The way our parents respond to our constant questioning plays a big part in how curious we continue to be, through adolescence and as adults. If our parents tend to ignore our questions and don't inspire us to keep questioning, eventually, we stop asking. If parents answer questions, they provide incentives for more questions and fuel curiosity. If parents answer questions with more questions, it pushes children to come up with their own answers and think for themselves.

Curiosity helps in keeping us from thinking we have all the answers and already know everything. It keeps us open to different perspectives of seeing the world. In this way curiosity

---

[6] Leslie, Ian. *Curious : the desire to know and why your future depends on it.* New York, NY: Basic Books, 2015. Print.

helps to develop two other qualities; open-mindedness and humility.

Open mindedness will keep your eyes open and your ears too. It will remind you that what we know individually, is insignificant compared to what we all know as a whole. That is also small, compared to all the things we still don't know. Accept that you don't have all the answers and neither does anyone else. You'll have to learn from many sources. Even then, you still won't know that much. That, should keep you humble.

Isidor Rabi won the Nobel Prize in physics, in 1944.

He was once asked,

"Why did you become a scientist, rather than a doctor or lawyer, like the other kids in your neighborhood?"

Rabi answered, "my mother made me a scientist. Every other Jewish mother in Brooklyn would ask her child after school: 'So? Did you learn anything today?' Not my mother. She always asked me a different question. 'Izzy,' she would say, 'did you ask a good question today?' That difference made me a scientist." [7]

You will find questions all over this book. They are meant to inspire you to think and search for answers which will lead you to ask more questions. That will push you to keep expanding as a person and always find something to be fascinated about. Even

---

[7] Burns, David B. "Did You Ask A Good Question Today?" *http://www.sdcity.edu*, 2009, www.sdcity.edu/portals/0/cms_editors/mesa/pdfs/researchacademy/didyouaskagoodquestiontoday.pdf.

more important, it will keep you open to all the possibilities you haven't considered.

Things to try:

- To keep yourself curious, ask questions and think of your own answers. Try explaining things to yourself first.
- Search for answers. Go to the library, search the internet, ask people. Ask everyone you know.
- Never stop questioning!
- Use diversive curiosity to find interesting things and then use epistemic curiosity to dig deeper.
- If you don't know, ask. It's better to not know and find out, than to pretend to know and stay ignorant. Be humble, ask, and stretch your mind.
- Ask why three times.
- Ask why not, what, what if, where, when, who, how.

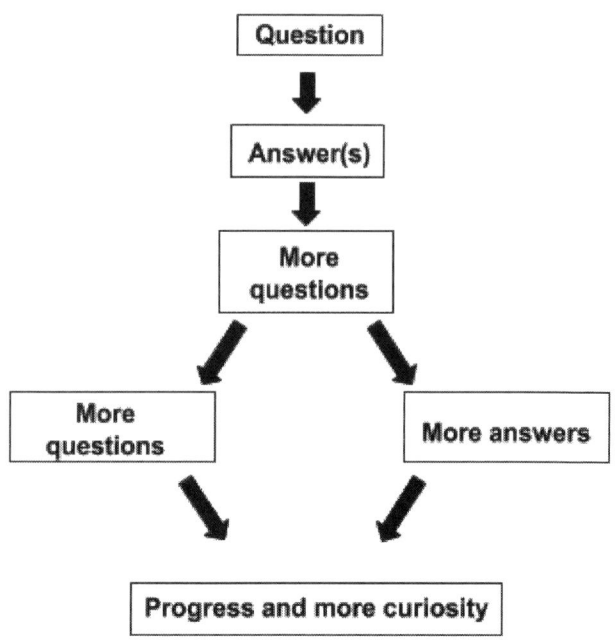

QUESTIONS

- What good questions did you ask today?
- What are you curious about and how can you learn more about it?
- Why are you curious about that?
- Who could this help?
- Are you curious enough?

List your models

Make a list of people you think have accomplished something meaningful in their lives. Pay special attention to the ones who have achieved what you want. *(A list to get you started is provided at the end of this book.)*

Things to try:

- Pick one person and study them. Learn all you can about them for one week or for one month. [8]
- Watch movies where there are characters you admire.
- Read books of successful people from the past and present and study their lives. Most will have stories filled with ups and downs. The stories of these people's lives, the untold ones, will inspire and encourage you when encountering obstacles on your path.
- Once you better understand these people, ask yourself the following questions.

QUESTIONS

- What would _____ do? How would _____ think about this issue? What would _____ not do?

---

[8] Altucher, James. *Reinvent Yourself.*, 2016. Print.

- Whose life can serve as an example to help you with what you're facing?
- What traits do you want to develop and what situations or experiences will force you to develop them?
- What traits do you need to develop and who can teach you them? Can you learn them in person, through a book, a video, a course?
- What has allowed this person to get to where they are?
- What characteristics do they have that I need? What are their strengths and weaknesses?
- What can you adopt as part of your own philosophy?

Mindfulness and breathing

"You practice mindfulness, on the one hand, to be calm and peaceful. On the other hand, as you practice mindfulness and live a life of peace, you inspire hope for a future of peace."

— Thich Nhat Hanh

Mindfulness means being present in the moment and paying attention to what is occurring. It makes you more sensitive to the context. You go from being on autopilot, to being self-aware. You can develop your level of mindfulness through meditation or breathing exercises.

Studies performed with people who meditate[9], show that meditation improves:

- Resilience
- Emotional regulation
- Perception, introspection and complex thinking
- Focus
- Pain tolerance
- Ability to learn from past experiences
- Decision making
- Performance

---

[9] *Mindfulness.* Boston, Massachusetts: Harvard Business Review Press, 2017. Print.

- Sense of compassion and kindness
- Ability to be less judgmental
- Creativity

Developing your ability to be mindful will allow you to go from participating in every one of your thoughts and getting lost in them, to being an observer and watching them go by. You'll feel more relaxed and be more present, in what you're doing.

To be more mindful:

- Sit or lie down in a comfortable position. Focus on your breathing. Try counting to five, as you breathe in and counting to ten, as you breathe out. If you lose focus, bring your attention back to your breathing
- Aim for 20-30 minutes every day. You can mix it up by doing a little in the morning, afternoon, and evening. Focus on your breathing before moving on to a different activity.
- Consider relaxing your whole body before you begin. Relax your head, then your shoulders, neck, arms, torso, and legs until you get down to your feet.
- Mindfulness meditation can also be done standing or walking. You can walk back and forth in the same space, focused on your breathing.
- The more you practice, the easier it gets to enter a mindful state and the more benefits you'll notice.
- Use a mindfulness bell every 30 minutes or 1 hour. When it rings, take a deep breath and be thankful for that moment in time. Be aware of your surroundings, the smell, sound, sight. Wherever you are, whatever you're doing, **be there**.

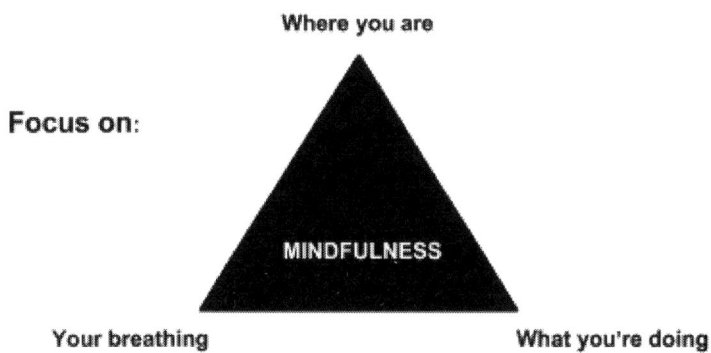

QUESTIONS

- Are you focused on the present moment? Are you really there, paying attention or is your attention somewhere else?
- How do you feel after spending time focusing on your breathing?
- Can I focus on my breathing at this moment to be more productive and feel more relaxed?
- When is the best time of day for you to work on breathing and meditation?

Taking immediate action

"When you know there's something you need to do, the biggest risk you can take is to do nothing at all."

-Anon

Start now and fix later. We avoid taking the first step because we're waiting for everything to be perfect, in order to start. Maybe we're waiting to have a plan for everything, to have everything set up, to consider all the different scenarios. We're waiting for the right time, we're waiting for everything to fall into place. We want more clarity, we want to learn more before we start because there's so much we still haven't learned. Then we'll get started. Eventually, we realize years have passed and we're in the exact same place because we haven't taken any action.

Sometimes, you've got to take a risk and build things along the way. You'll never have all the information to make the perfect decision (if that exists at all). Make a decision, take action, implement, and adjust your sails along the way. The distance from point A to point B is shortest, if you travel in a straight line. In terms of time, however, it may take longer.

Sometimes we go around in circles, but those circles are actually taking us closer to point b. As long as you're taking action, you're going to learn along the way, and figure things out. The longer you wait to get started, the more things that'll hold you back.

Family, debt, mortgage, insurance, and utility bills will add to the pile of things you have to think about. Although it's still possible to act in that situation, it'll be harder.

Once you take action and get going, you'll begin to create momentum. That momentum will help you develop competence and confidence and they will feed off each other. More action, more competence, more confidence, more belief that it is possible. Every step will get you closer. Every step will also test you and cause frustration. See it as part of the process of moving towards what you want. Learn to expect frustration and remember, *"This too shall pass."*

Anything can be learned and whether or not you have talent, is not important. What matters is that you're willing to work at it. So if you're putting in the effort, learning from mistakes along the way, why would you not be able to get there?

Things to try:

- The 5 second rule. Count from 5 to 1. Then act despite any fear or resistance you may feel. Counting down from 5 to 1 doesn't give you enough time to talk yourself out of it.[10]
- Understand that the "right" time may never come. Now is the best time. You will never be younger than this moment.

---

[10] Robbins, Mel. *The 5 second rule : transform your life, work, and confidence with everyday courage.* Place of publication not identified: Savio Republic, 2017. Print.

- Stop basing your decisions on feelings. First decide, then act, then feel.[11]
- If you want to change how you feel, you first have to change your behavior.
- Remember that you control your beliefs, your actions, and your effort.

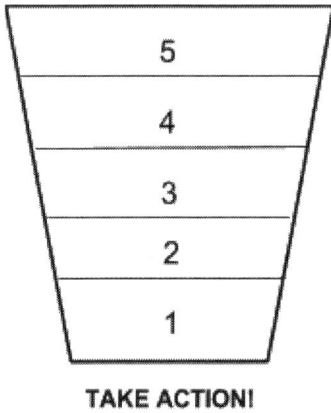

TAKE ACTION!

---

[11] Voogd, Peter. *6 Months to 6 Figures: "the Fastest Way to Get from Where You Are to Where You Want to Be Regardless of the Economy"*. , 2016. Print.

QUESTIONS

- What do I need to do for the outcome I desire, to be inevitable?
- Am I taking daily action to create the life I want or am I looking for excuses to postpone action?
- Do I have enough information to act now or is there something real that holds me back?
- Who can I ask for help? Who can help hold me accountable?

Discipline, consistency, and focus

"Discipline yourself, and others won't need to."
— John Wooden

Without discipline and focus, it is difficult to get anywhere. Consistent discipline and consistent focus on the right actions. That will make you unstoppable. Lionel Messi, Michael Jordan, Roger Federer, Bobby Fischer, Bill Gates, Warren Buffett, Pablo Picasso, Salvador Dali, how did they do it?

Talent? A focus on their strengths? A good understanding of themselves? Maybe. But perhaps what made the biggest difference of all, is the amount of time spent working on their craft, with consistent discipline. Maybe that's what allowed them to reach a level few attain.

QUESTIONS

- What are you focused on?
- Are you consistently working towards it?
- Do you have the discipline to do it, day in and day out?

CONSISTENCY

Show up every day. Whatever you do, keep your feet moving. Consistently push forward. Push on, push on, and push on.

Bruce Lee said, *"I fear not the man who has practiced 10,000 kicks once, but I fear the man who has practiced one kick 10,000 times."*

Consistency is practicing one kick 10,000 times. That's how you build competence and eventually, mastery.

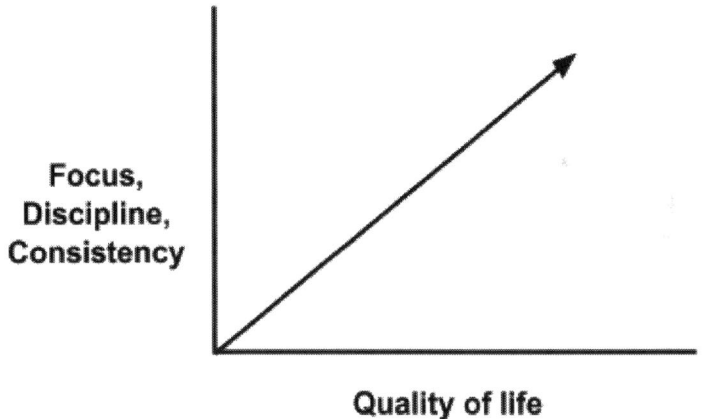

FOCUS

*"It is during our darkest moments that
we must focus to see the light."*

–Aristotle

Focus isn't just about concentrating, but about being present in the moment. Having the ability to pay attention to what you're doing despite what's happening around you.

When you're fully focused on the present moment, your performance improves, you're better able to respond, and you gain more insight. You're better able to enter what athletes call, "the zone." Focus helps develop your skills and awareness. This means you can picture future scenarios and self-reflect.

Most of the day we're distracted by a variety of tasks. Especially, when multitasking. We are focused on one thing at a time, only a small part of our day. What if we flipped that around and spent most of our day focused on a single task and were distracted only for short moments, at a time?

Things to try:

- Plan your rest time and your work time. Have a set time to stop working.
- Focus only on one thing, at a time.
- Focus on what you *do want* in your life, not on what you don't.
- Do the most urgent and the most important things first. Always!

- Use meditation in order to develop your focus.
- Try a mindfulness bell every certain amount of time.
- Develop your own routine to improve your focus.
- Stay away from email, telephones, social media, and other people while you're working on your most important tasks.
- Take breaks often, get up and get your body moving.
- Work towards your goals every day.
- Set apart time to just rest, disconnect, and let go.
- Avoid multitasking.
- Take an internet break.
- Do the most important thing at the same time, every day.

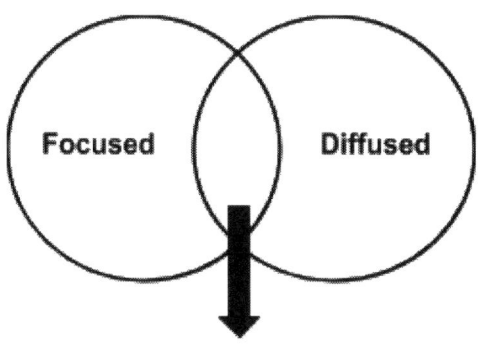

A better approach to learning

Focusing with time management

A good way to focus is by managing your time. Use the time of day when your focus, energy, and productivity are at their highest, to work on your most important and urgent work.

To figure out when you're most productive, keep track of energy, focus, and productivity levels at different hours of the day. Give each area a rating of 1 (low) to 5 (high). Do this for a couple of weeks. If you keep a regular schedule, you'll start to see strong patterns and specific hours when you're most focused and have high energy levels. Use that time for your most important work.

Take all the things you have to do and divide them using the '*Eisenhower Matrix.*' [12]

Important and urgent	Important but not urgent
Not important but urgent	Not important and not urgent

---

[12] Krogerus, Mikael, et al. *The decision book : fifty models for strategic thinking.* New York: W. W. Norton & Company, 2018. Print.

- **Important and urgent**- Do these first
- **Important, but not urgent**- Plan a time to do them
- **Not important, but urgent**- Can someone else do it? If so, delegate.
- **Not important and not urgent**- Is it necessary to do it? If not, let it go.

*** Make sure to clearly decide what you have to do. Write it out and set a specific amount of time necessary to complete that task. Make sure to give it enough time.

Try these ideas as well:

- Let go, rest, take a break, go for a walk
- Focus only on one thing at a time
- 80-20 Principle - focus on the most valuable 20% of actions, that creates 80% of the results

QUESTIONS

- When is your focus stronger and weaker? How can you make it stronger?
- Can you plan your day better to stay more focused? Can you also benefit from resting and disconnecting?
- Are you disciplined enough to do the same thing every day, around the same time, in order to develop the

necessary consistency? How can you make sure you stick with this?
- Who can hold you accountable?
- What if you planned your day the night before?

Go Pro

"Good things come to those who work,
not those who wait."

—Tim Grover
(Trainer to Michael Jordan, Kobe Bryant,
and Dwyane Wade among others)

If you look in the mirror right now, would you call yourself an amateur or a professional?

What are the differences?

The amateur puts in a minimum number of hours and is only looking to have fun. The amateur doesn't measure or use their time well. They tend to waste most of their time on mindless tasks that aren't going to get them any closer to where they want to be. The amateur treats their work as a hobby and only does it when they feel like it. The amateur doesn't plan and isn't ready for the unexpected. The amateur doesn't go all the way.

The professional jumps in and tries to learn as much as possible. The professional is humble and admits when they don't know. The professional looks for stories, biographies and learns from those who came before and were able to achieve what they want. The professional comes up with different ideas to try and immediately puts them into action.

The professional learns and implements. The professional fails often, reflects, learns lessons, and keeps going. The professional knows that mistakes are experience and that it adds up in value. The professional keeps going despite the obstacles. They plan ahead and take it seriously. They spend their time wisely and go all the way. The professional finds fulfillment in putting in the work.

Are you a professional or an amateur?

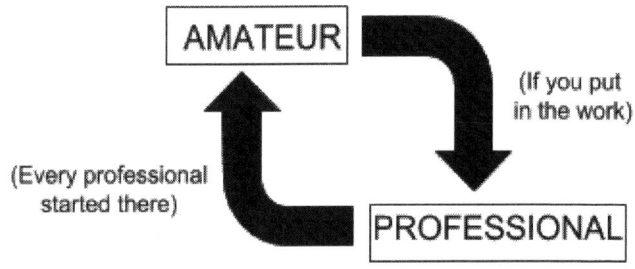

"Turning pro is a mindset. If we are struggling with fear, self-sabotage, procrastination, self-doubt, etc., the problem is, we're thinking like amateurs. Amateurs don't show up. Amateurs crap out. Amateurs let adversity defeat them. The pro thinks differently. He shows up, he does his work, he keeps on truckin', no matter what."

-Steven Pressfield

Love the work

If you're a professional, then you have to get comfortable with the grind. Working hard is not something that requires skill or talent. It does require time, sacrifice, and a strong focus on what matters.

The only way we can get better is to practice. To train. To constantly put in the hours. To get up early and work late. By following this path you will get to what Maslow called, unconscious competence.

<u>*Abraham Maslow's Four Stages of Competence*</u>

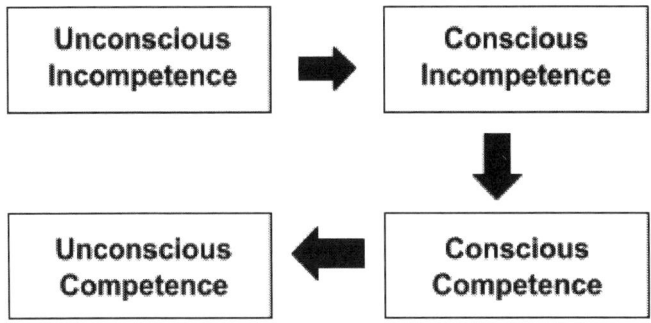

- Stage 1 - Unconscious incompetence = You don't know that you don't know.
- Stage 2 - Conscious incompetence = You know you don't know.

- Stage 3- Conscious competence = You know that you know.
- Stage 4- Unconscious competence = You know without thinking about it. It becomes second nature.

When accepting to mentor her, Coach James Galanis told female soccer star, Carli Lloyd,

"A regular person works nine to five okay... And at five o'clock, they shut down. They have beers. They do whatever it is they want. The rest of the world has an off switch that happens every day, but there's no off switch for you. Your off switch comes at the end of your career. From this point on, the switch is on and it doesn't come off until you take your boots off and you've retired from the game." [13]

That's what it takes to perform at a level where everything you do, looks like it's easy. People only see the tip of the iceberg, but never see the enormous bottom submerged in water; the time spent in solitude, the amount of frustration, the dedication, the love for the craft, the ups and downs, and the sacrifices.

QUESTIONS

- If you took one thing and practiced it for 1, 2, 3 or more hours, every single day, where would you be in one year?

---

[13] Bercovici, Jeff. *Play on : the new science of elite performance at any age.* Boston: Houghton Mifflin Harcourt, 2018. Print.

- What skills do you currently have and what stage of competence are they in?
- How could you take them to the next stage? What new challenge can you create for yourself?

The process is the way

We focus on the results; the end goal. What if we focused on the process?

When we consider the end goal it seems exciting and worthwhile. The anticipation of that end goal brings us pleasure. The anticipation is born in the process. When you achieve a goal, you celebrate and that's it, you move on. The process is where you spend most of your time. The hours of practicing, being uncomfortable, and getting frustrated is part of the cycle of moving towards mastery.

If we're focused on the goal and haven't yet arrived at our destination, we get impatient and allow negative thoughts in our head.

We have to fall in love with the process. At first, we don't know how and that's frustrating. But we can use that frustration to develop curiosity. That's how we figure out how to change something that's not working. Then we make the adjustment, improve, and the process repeats itself. This time, with a higher aim.

The more frustration you go through, the more opportunity you have for greater amounts of happiness, joy and pleasure. The more frustration you try to avoid, the more frustration you'll feel. Avoiding frustration and discomfort doesn't bring pleasure. It brings boredom, routine and resentment. It's like trying to obtain a reward, by taking zero risk.

Frustration or failure means you have not achieved a certain level of competence in an area. You need to become more competent. To determine the area where you need to be more competent, constantly look for feedback, self-assess, and seek criticism more than praise.

Focusing on the process every day, will reinforce your belief that you can get what you want. You'll know you're headed in the right direction. If you just focus on the end result and realize you're still not there, (and that is all you see), you'll be let down.

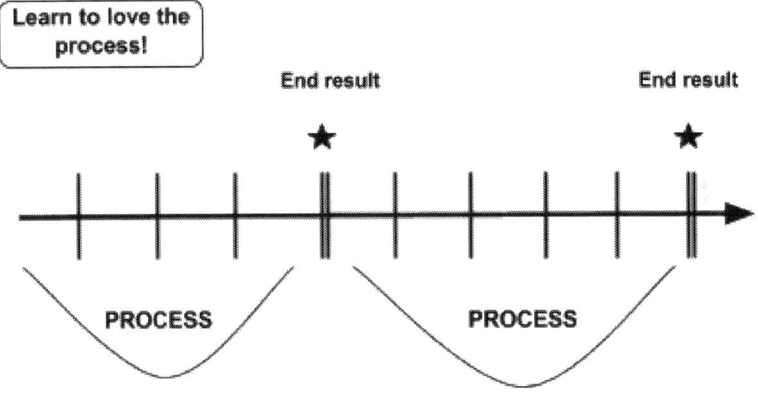

QUESTIONS

- What if all you have to do is spend 4 hours every single day working on a few specific tasks, consistently, every day. That's it! Could you do it? Would you do it?

- Are you doing what you need to do, every day, to hit your weekly goal?
- Are you on track with weekly goals in order to hit your monthly goal?
- Are you on track with your monthly goal in order to hit the quarterly or yearly goal?
- Consistently measure and track where you are. Ask others for help.
- Are you doing enough or not enough? Are you close to where you thought you'd be? Are you far away?
- What do you need to adjust?

Constant growth

No matter how small the step, take it consistently. Many small steps create a ripple effect that compounds. Like a drop of water in a calm pond, it spreads. The benefit of small steps is that the resistance they encounter, is low.

As time passes we are constantly growing. Growing in age, experience, knowledge, everything. How we grow and the speed at which it occurs, is partly, in our control.

Learning is part of our everyday lives. Whatever we do, we're going through the process of learning. Learning to walk, to talk, to feed ourselves, to read and write, different subjects and languages, driving, managing a budget, getting a job, etc.

It's all a constant process of learning and getting better at what we do and how we do it. It's a process that is always evolving. There is no end. No conclusion. It's a continuum. Just as the universe is expanding and moving further out, we should do the same. If not, we start to think in terms of conclusions and think we already have the answers. When we do that, we close ourselves off to possibility, discovery, and the unknown.

Things to try:

- Learn something new every day.
- Read a book, watch some useful educational videos, take a free online course from a university.

- Try something you've never done before
- Apply your new skills. Put them to work for you.
- Teach someone something useful.

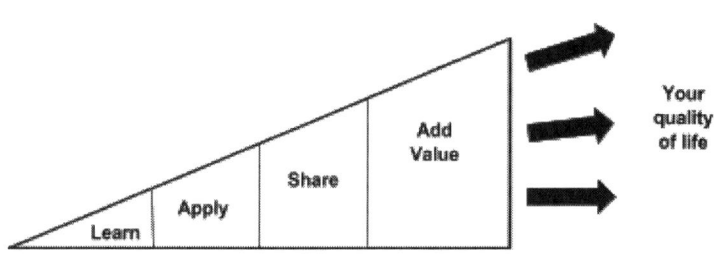

QUESTIONS

- Are you improving a bit each day? Learning and implementing new skills and tools every day?
- If your effort compounds, what will that mean in one month, one year or five?
- What are the skills you need to improve on?
- What can you do to learn them? How will you practice them? For how long and at what time of day? What do you expect to happen?
- Do you enjoy what you do? Do you like the person you're becoming?
- What specifically do you not enjoy about what you do?
- Are you building your competence or hurting it? Are you building your confidence or hurting it?
- What action can you take daily that provides the most value? How can you get the most from your training?

- Who can help you on this path and provide feedback and training?
- Is there a teacher or mentor that can help you get there and can open doors for you? Can they introduce you to others who are on the same path and who would be willing to train with you?

Challenge, ability, and flow

Psychologist, Mihaly Csikszentmihalyi, states that *"flow"* [14] is achieved by:

- Being focused on the present moment,
- on an activity we choose
- That is not too easy, and not too difficult. The challenge level is just right for our level of ability.
- There is a clear objective.
- We receive instant feedback.
- While performing the activity we lose our sense of time, forget ourselves, and feel a deep sense of satisfaction. This is what athletes call *"being in the zone."*

To achieve flow, improve your ability in something you enjoy. Make the challenge more difficult. Play or compete with someone whose ability level is a bit higher than yours. This way you challenge yourself to improve. Avoid challenges that are too difficult as you may get the urge to give up. By following this path, you'll be moving out of your comfort zone, learning new things, and maintaining a high level of interest. You'll create *"flow"* in your life and continue to seek new challenges.

---

[14] Csikszentmihalyi, Mihaly. *Flow : the psychology of optimal experience*. New York: Harper & Row, 1990. Print

Things to try:

- Think of the areas in your life that are important to you (health, work, relationships, spirituality, your children, partner, and a hobby). Create challenges for each one that will force you to keep growing.

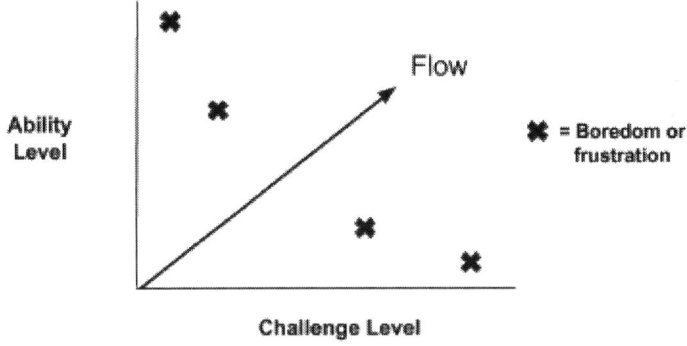

"If we know what that set point is, we can predict fairly accurately when you will be in flow, and it will be when your challenges are higher than average and skills are higher than average."

-Mihaly Csikszentmihalyi

QUESTIONS

- What activity has given you a feeling of flow?
- What areas do you have ability in? What is challenging for you?
- What brings you fulfillment or satisfaction?

- What comes relatively easy to you that you haven't paid attention to?
- What can you spend hours talking about or doing, without noticing that lots of time has passed?
- When you feel frustrated, could it be your ability is not developed enough to deal with the challenge? Or is it that the challenge is too easy for your ability level and you feel under challenged and bored?

PART 2 - THE WHEEL OF EMOTIONS

"A gem cannot be polished without friction, nor a man perfected without trials."

–Seneca

Figuring out your emotions so you can move forward

The better you understand what you're going through emotionally, the easier it will be to move forward. If you don't know what's bothering you and avoid thinking about it, you'll end up miserable and so will everyone around you. No one likes to spend time with people like that.

Write stuff down. *"Morning pages"*, an exercise Julia Cameron discusses in, *The right to write*,[15] is a great way to let everything out of your system. You do this by writing 3 pages nonstop; without editing, in a stream of consciousness style, first thing every morning. It will force you to put it all down on paper and release whatever is on your mind. You can then go through it and read it or simply forget about it.

I have found that it tires out your mind of all the chatter. It may or may not make much sense as it is all a stream of consciousness, but the point is not an award winning novel. It's to work through your issues on a piece of paper. You could alternately do so by composing a piece of music on the spot and recording it. You could paint something or draw something. You could dance something and film it.

---

[15] Cameron, Julia. *The right to write : an invitation and initiation into the writing life*. New York: Jeremy P. Tarcher/Putnam, 1998. Print.

Whatever you do, do something to deal with your emotions, feelings and what you're going through. Psychologists are useful and can ask questions that help you discover things about yourself that you hadn't considered. Sometimes we simply need someone to listen. If you need a person to do this, try going to a counselor, a community group, therapy or a trusted friend. Make sure the person is neutral and has your best interest in mind.

As you go through life, you'll encounter a variety of different feelings. You'll feel fear, rejection, frustration, pain, sadness, helplessness, lost, and more. Learn to expect all this.

To determine how you're feeling it helps to have a list of basic emotions that we can feel. By seeing the names of the emotions, we're better able to pinpoint what and how we feel. You can use Robert Plutchik's 'Wheel of emotions,'[16] (in the image), to determine where you are.

The main emotions Plutchik identified are:

- Joy and sadness
- Trust and disgust
- Fear and anger
- Surprise and anticipation

---

[16] Hokuma. "Plutchik's Wheel of Emotions: What is it and How to Use it in Counseling?" *Positive Psychology Program*, 24 Dec. 2017, positivepsychologyprogram.com/emotion-wheel/.

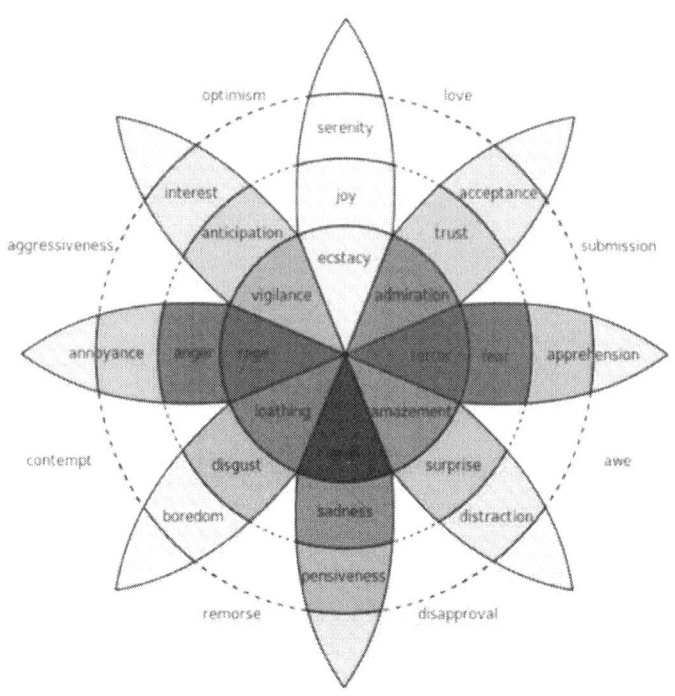

Image credit: Déjà vu — Machine Elf 1735 (talk) 19:29, 23 April 2010 (UTC)

The closer to the center of the wheel, the more intense the emotion. The colors represent similar emotions. The emotions on the outside, with no color, result when two primary emotions mix. The polar opposite of each emotion is across from it.

Use Plutchik's wheel to first identify what emotions you're feeling. Then determine how intense they are. Are there any primary emotions mixing that are causing other emotions to pop up? What events in your life are contributing to this? What can you do to move away from the emotion you don't want?

Take a look at your morning pages for more insight. Once you determine what you feel, pay more attention to those emotions. In what way can you work your way through them or use them to your advantage?

Consider tracking different feelings during the day for a couple of weeks. What do you generally feel in the morning, afternoon and evening? Is there a pattern? What are the most dominant feelings and what triggers them? What are the feelings you don't want and what triggers them? How can you prevent those from occurring more often?

How can you create more positive feelings?

Things to try:

- Morning pages
- Use Plutchik's wheel to identify what you feel and use it to your benefit
- In the following chapters, you'll find ways to cope with the negative emotions of fear, sadness, frustration, and anger. Use the exercises.

QUESTIONS

- What are you feeling right now? What if you wrote down your thoughts in a stream of consciousness without editing? Might it help uncover what is going on inside and therefore help to move forward?
- What if you embrace how you feel and ask why you may be feeling that way? Using your curiosity, try substituting it with another feeling.

PART 3- PUTTING LIFE'S CHALLENGES IN PERSPECTIVE

PARADOX

Tao Te Ching #2 – Lao Zi

"When people see some things as beautiful,
Other things become ugly.
When people see some things as good,
Other things become bad.
Being and non-being create each other.
Difficult and easy support each other.
Long and short define each other.
High and low depend on each other.
Before and after follow each other.
Therefore the Master acts without doing anything
And teaches without saying anything.
Things arise and she lets them come;
Things disappear and she lets them go.
She has but doesn't possess,
Acts but doesn't expect.
When her work is done, she forgets it.
That is why it lasts forever."

–Translation by Stephen Mitchell [17]

---

[17] Laozi, and Stephen Mitchell. *Tao Te Ching: A New English Version*. New York: HarperCollins, 2006. Print.

Yin and Yang

The *Tao Te Ching* #2, by Lao Zi, explains the concept of paradox. The light, when not present, creates darkness. Happiness, when absent, creates sadness. Day becomes night and night becomes day.

In Taoism, this concept is known as Yin and Yang. It refers to the duality and unity present in everything. The following are some of the principles in yin and yang:

- Yin and yang are opposites. They are also interdependent. (Light is the opposite of dark. In the darkness, however, there can still be light.)
- Yin and yang can be subdivided. (For example, sadness can divide into depression (yin) or mild discontent (yang).)
- When one increases, the other decreases. (An increase in pleasure, creates a decrease in pain.)
- Yin and yang can transform into their opposites. (Night turns into day, and day into night.)
- In yin, there is yang and in yang, there is yin. (When sad, there is still something that makes you happy.)
- Yin and yang are relative. (What is good for you, may be bad for another. It depends on your perspective.)

Pain, suffering, and joy

All the pain, the sorrow, and the discomfort we feel, makes us stronger. This is difficult to accept whenever we go through difficult situations. Often, we get stuck and see no way of getting out. We go around in circles, deceiving ourselves into thinking we're going somewhere, when in reality, we're headed nowhere.

To develop your ability to handle pain, first make the choice to be tough and to withstand the difficulties life throws at you. Then act the part. You must go through situations that force you to be a tougher person. This way, you develop the skill through real experience.

Pain brings with it pleasure. Sorrow and joy come hand in hand. Whatever happens, you can learn something from it and be better for it. How you respond to situations that affect your life, will determine whether or not they benefit you.

The guitar is made from the wood of a tree. Before it can be a musical instrument and produce beautiful melodies, the tree must be cut down, dried, cut into pieces and reshaped. The wood gets sanded, painted, varnished, and nuts and bolts are attached to it. All the parts are glued together and left to dry. The strings are placed and then tuned. Finally, you can play the finished guitar, and if you know how, you can make amazing music. The wood had to go through the pain of being chopped down, cut, sliced and carved, to get to the pleasure of making sweet melodies.

The four noble truths that Buddha taught were: [18]

1. The truth of suffering – There is suffering in life from the beginning to the end.

2. The truth of the origin of suffering– The reason for our suffering is desire.

3. The truth of the ending of suffering – Suffering can be ended by detaching from desire and attachment.

4. The truth of the path to the ending of suffering – There is a path that eliminates suffering.

If you are trying to avoid misery, you'll end up experiencing misery. In order to put an end to it, you have to face it and accept it. We tend to shoot ourselves with two arrows, as Thich Nhat Hanh says, in *No mud, No lotus*.[19] The first arrow is a situation that causes us pain and suffering; the loss of a loved one, the ending of a relationship, the failure of achieving a dream. The second arrow, is due to our beliefs. We over exaggerate the pain and suffering and create a domino effect of negativity. As Hanh says, *"we need to learn to stop shooting ourselves with the second arrow."*

First, you have to realize that happiness cannot exist without suffering. Both of these things are only momentary. They do not last forever. They are constantly working together.

---

[18] Buckingham, Will. *The Philosophy Book: [big Ideas Simply Explained]*. London: DK Pub, 2011. Print.

[19] Hạnh, Nhất. *No mud, no lotus : the art of transforming suffering*. New Delhi: Aleph Book Company, 2017. Print.

Every day, as Hanh says, *"Every birthday we celebrate life, we also celebrate death and the passing of time. They are happening together, at the same time...The flower when it wilts, becomes the compost. The compost can help grow a flower again."*

The rain, the clouds, the sunshine are not the flower, but they are part of what helps the flower, become a flower. Without these, there wouldn't be a flower.

Our suffering also comes from our resistance. As Osho says in, *The art of living and dying,*[20] "*the pain often disappears if you flow with it.*"

How can we do that?

- When you feel pain or suffering, use statements like:

    1. "Such are things."
    2. "Such is the way of the body."
    3. "Hello my suffering, I know you are there."
    4. "Good morning my pain, I see you. I am here. Don't worry."
    5. "This too shall pass."

- Locate the pain, sit in silence and just observe it. The more you look at it, the stronger the feeling and the easier you will see where it's located. Oftentimes, it disappears after

---

[20] Osho. *The art of living and dying*. London: Watkins Publishing, 2013. Print.

this. The cause of the pain may reveal itself to you. If it comes back, repeat the process.
- Practice letting go. What would happen if you lost all the things you consider to be important and necessary to live your life?
- Concentrate. Focus on the moment. If you find yourself focusing on the past or other things that are not occurring or going to occur, be thankful that you are not in that situation.
- Practice meditation and breathing.

Happiness and sadness

> *"Very little is needed to make a happy life; it is all within yourself, in your way of thinking."*
>
> – Marcus Aurelius

Some days you'll feel happy, others you'll be sad. During the day you'll also fluctuate. Neither will last forever and the more things you do that bring you joy, the more chance you have to return to that state. Thich Nhat Hanh says, *"nothing can survive without food, including happiness."* This is true of sadness as well; we prolong negative feelings by adding wood to the fire.

There are going to be times when you're feeling great, plowing forward, no matter what, and everything seems to work out right for you. There will be times that are the exact opposite. These times will be difficult and challenging, but they'll also teach you. They will open the door to opportunities that you didn't know existed and allow you to keep growing.

Some ideas to try from, *No mud, No lotus*:

- Practice letting go. What you think you need for survival gets in the way of happiness. Write down the things you believe are necessary for you to live well. Let go of one. Then let go of another.
- Pay attention to the positive things in your life. Focus on them.
- Practice meditation and being present.

- Write down all the reasons you have for being happy at this moment. Don't stop until you run out of ideas.
- Think back on difficult situations in your life and be thankful you're no longer in that position.

Also consider these coping mechanisms: [21]

- Participating in activities that make you feel good.
- Using humor to take life less seriously and laugh at yourself
- Spending time with pets
- Reframe how you view the situation or reframe the sadness.
- Spend time alone and dig into what you're feeling.

---

[21] Sadness." *Wikipedia, the Free Encyclopedia*, Wikimedia Foundation, Inc, 27 June 2018, en.wikipedia.org/wiki/Sadness. Accessed 27 July 2018.

Fear and courage

"Life shrinks or expands in proportion to one's courage."

-Anais Nin

What causes the most fear is the thought of fear itself. The thought creates feelings and that creates the tension we feel within.

Seneca said, *"You act like mortals in all that you fear and like immortals in all you desire."*

We postpone taking action on what we want, as if we're going to live forever. We're scared to take action because we fear death. Instead of letting the fear gain power over you, focus on increasing courage. Take daily actions to face what you fear and build courage in that area.

You can use exposure therapy. You slowly expose yourself to your fear. Let's say you're afraid of the open water. What could you do to slowly let go of this fear? How about starting by watching videos about life at sea. Try reading a book or watching a documentary on someone who sailed the world on their own. That way you can see the beauty you are missing out on. Watch footage of scuba divers. You could try snorkeling in the beach next time you go, near the shore. Try swimming with dolphins. Each step you take is building your courage and you're then able to move onto something more challenging. Consider learning to scuba dive and then going for a few dives. Try learning to surf and sail. How about participating in a swimming competition at sea or swimming across the English Channel? Do it slowly, no need to rush. Enjoy each step along the way.

By taking this path, courage and incredible experiences will substitute your fear. You'll gain confidence and that will create more courage. Then you can tackle another fear.

Things to try:

- Think of how you can develop more courage in the areas you fear. Make lists of things you could do that would slowly immerse you into that situation. You don't have to jump in head first. Just put your feet in.
- Make a list of the things that scare you and make you feel uncomfortable and then take one step, every day, to slowly build courage in those areas.
- Join a support group, get a mentor, join a community and have people hold you accountable.
- Learn to roll with the punches. Whatever gets thrown at you, be able to go with it. In improv comedy you learn two words to avoid, *"no"* and *"but."* Substitute them with "*yes, and*". Whatever someone says to you, is an invitation. Be able to take the invitation that somebody throws at you and go with the flow. Add to it. Play with it. Add your own ingredients to the recipe.

Also try these ideas from *The art of mental training*,[22] by D.C. Gonzalez:

- When fear comes into your mind, interrupt it immediately. Focus on your breathing.
- Ask yourself where this fear is coming from?
- Substitute the negative thoughts for positive images and self-talk. Think of your positive past experiences.

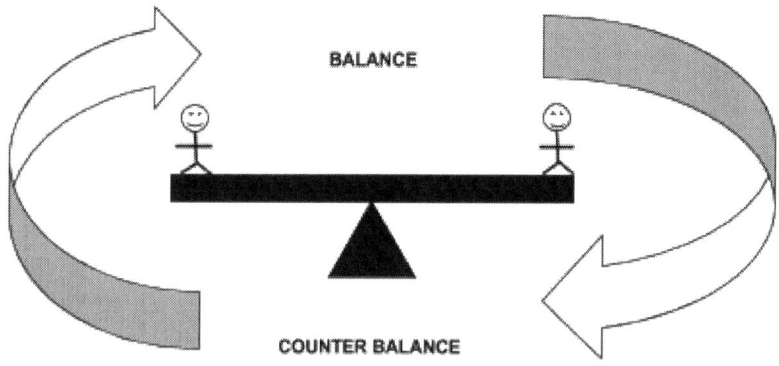

*"Without counter balance the see-saw doesn't rock.

---

[22] Gonzalez, Daniel C, and Alice McVeigh. *The Art of Mental Training: A Guide to Performance Excellence*. S. l.: GonzoLane Media, 2013. Print

QUESTIONS

- What are some areas in your life where you can see the paradox?
- Where have you focused your attention on one side, without seeing the benefit of the other side?
- How have these ideas changed your perspective and how you view different situations in your life?
- Why do you think this is useful? Where will you apply this? What situations will benefit from this idea if you apply it right now?

*"It is not death that a man should fear,
but he should fear never beginning to live."*

–Marcus Aurelius

CONTEXT

How it all makes sense

Philosopher, Alan Watts, believed that when we look at something, there is a difference in point of view, depending on the magnification. There is a big difference between looking at something through a microscope, with the naked eye, and through a telescope.

Watts said, *"if you take a newspaper photograph and look at it through the naked eye, it looks like a human face. If you place it under a microscope you'll see dots scattered meaninglessly all over the place. If you step away, however, you will begin to see patterns emerge. The dots add up to something. What at one level was conflict, becomes harmony at a higher level."* [23]

Perhaps this is what's happening in our lives. When we look at a situation at one level, it looks like conflict and doesn't make any sense. At a higher level, it makes all the sense in the world.

This is present everywhere we look in nature. Every situation we're in. When things happen, we're often caught by surprise and don't know why they happened. It seems to not make any sense at all. As time goes by, things become clearer, and we're able to see how it's all part of the bigger picture.

---

[23] Watts, Alan. "Alan Watts ~ It All Makes Sense." *YouTube*, 21 Mar. 2017, youtu.be/zUXtraKXOz8.

The concept of tension and release is used in music to create interest and variety. Tension can be created through the repetition of notes, gradually changing from soft to loud, changes in tempo from slow to fast, using a specific rhythm, or notes that are dissonant when played together. All these techniques create a feeling of tension in both the music and listener. The tension builds up and creates anticipation for the final release. That final release, is harmony.

Life is a constant cycle of tension and release and conflict and harmony. We have to learn to navigate both sides.

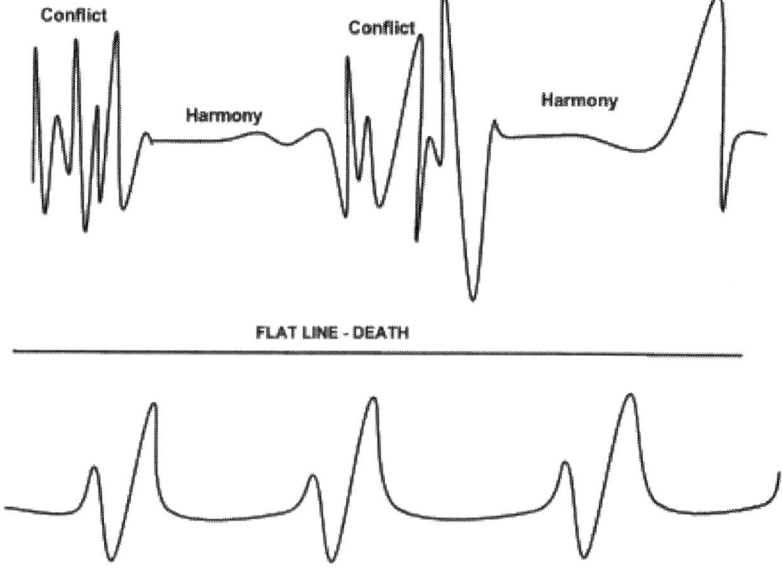

A beating heart = You're alive. The ebb and flow makes life exciting.

QUESTIONS

- Can you see how different situations in your life are\ were connected in a larger way? How it is all part of the whole?
- Has this helped you look at things in a different way?
- Describe conflict in your life and how it turned into harmony? Can you see how tension and release is a natural path of life? Where is there tension in your life? What do you think will result from the tension?
- How may the current conflicts you have, lead to harmony? How may this current harmony end up in conflict and how can you prepare for it?

The details, bigger picture, going deep, and applying wide

In stock trading, traders make decisions to buy and sell, based on price action. They look at charts that track the changing price of a stock, over time. There are different timeframes to view price action. You can look at a daily chart, where each bar on a chart, represents one full day. There are hourly charts, where each bar is equal to one hour. Many traders use the multiple time frames approach. Once they determine there's an opportunity to buy or sell a stock, they look at other time frames. These other time frames provide context and a better entry and exit point.

One trader, for example, sees an opportunity to buy XYZ stock at 10$, on a daily chart. This would be the equivalent of being focused on the details. The trader moves to a weekly chart and zooms out. She does this to get context and asks these types of questions:

- What has the overall trend been in the last few weeks and months?
- Does this look like a good moment to buy?
- Is there something that I've not seen, missed or don't know?

This zoomed out view, at a higher time frame, provides the bigger picture.

Once the trader concludes that the big picture supports the trade, she goes down to an even lower time frame. In this case it may be an hourly chart. The trader will use that time frame, to determine the best moment and price, to enter the trade. This is the equivalent of going deeper into the detail, seeing each one as a world of its own, and then making decisions based on that.

"Can't see the forest, for the trees." That is commonly stated when you can't see the bigger picture. You only focus on what's in front of you. You forget about the larger picture and get lost in the details. In every situation or problem you encounter, you'll benefit from using the multiple perspective approach.

In *Make your brain smarter*, Dr. Sandra Chapman discusses ways to integrate new information to better understand and apply it.[24]

Zoom in on the details; go deeper than usual. Understand the facts and what the issue is, up close. Once you've seen everything in detail, zoom out. Look at things from a birds eye view. When you view things from this larger perspective, you'll see what's important, knowable, urgent, unknown, and within your control. That way, you'll know where to pay attention. Being able to zoom out allows you to put things in perspective. To take all the facts and details and extract major ideas.

Once you determine major ideas, think of ways to apply widely. This means taking the concepts and the learning from one area

---

[24] Chapman, Sandra B., and Shelly Kirkland. *Make your brain smarter : increase your brain's creativity, energy, and focus.* New York: Free Press, 2013. Print.

and applying it to different areas. That way, you can come up with innovative solutions and applications.

Things to try:

- Take any challenging situation in your life. Write out the details, then zoom out and look at it from a distance.
- Think of solutions from different areas and how they could be applied.
- Consider if there are any other experiences you can draw from that could be applied here. Think of how you may be able to apply these ideas in other areas. Consider the longer term consequences. Consider the odds.
- Take the opposite path. Focus on the "is not". Pay attention to what's not there. What is not said, what is not acted out. We tend to pay attention to what is and not what isn't.

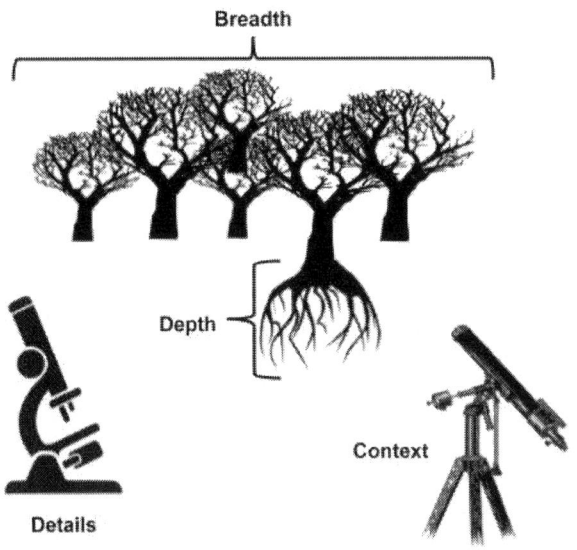

QUESTIONS

- When you look at the details of a situation, what do you see? What do you see when you take a look at the big picture?
- Have you noticed something new? Was there something missing? What does the context tell you?
- How might it be helpful to look at different situations this way?
- Are there ideas from different areas that you can use and that work well here?
- How could you go deeper into this issue and discover new things?

Re-framing perspectives

Look at a situation, receive the same information as others, but be able to come up with different conclusions. This is called the framing effect. It gives you the ability to use the insight of multiple perspectives. To view situations from different angles that you hadn't considered.

Take this statement: *"You don't love me because you yell at me."*

There are many different possibilities for this statement.

- Yelling at you could mean I simply had a rough day at work and unfortunately, took my anger out on you.
- Is there a possibility that yelling at you, means I love you? Perhaps I care so much, that by yelling, I thought my message would get across.
- Does this mean you (other person) don't love me because last week you yelled at me when I forgot to wash the dishes?
- Does not yelling at each other, equal love?
- What will you think of this when you're 90? Will yelling still mean I don't love you? What if you're going deaf?

You could continue to produce many different frames for this statement.

You can't control what others conclude, but you can use the power of multiple perspectives to come to your own conclusions and determine what is most useful. The more frames you can come up with, the better your ability to adjust to circumstances and frame situations in ways that benefit you and other people.

There is an old story of a Chinese farmer and his horse.

The horse runs away and the farmer's neighbors come by to say, *"that's too bad"* to which he responds, *"maybe."*

The horse returns the next day with two other wild horses. The neighbors come by to say, *"how lucky"* to which he also responds, *"maybe."*

The next day his son falls and breaks his leg, trying to ride one of the wild horses. Again, the neighbors say, *"that's too bad."* He answers, "*maybe.*"

The next day the army comes into town to recruit soldiers. The farmer's son is not recruited due to his broken leg. The neighbors all say, *"how fortunate."*

You already know what the farmer responds.

You choose what meaning events have in your life. They can be bad, good, or just...maybe.

In *Mindlines,*[25] by Michael Hall, he says, *"context changes the meaning. Different meanings lead to different responses which lead to different emotions."*

Avoid seeing crises as insurmountable problems. You can't change the fact that highly stressful events happen, but you can change the meaning you give these events. Then you'll be better able to respond. Look beyond the present and see how future circumstances may be better because of your current circumstances.

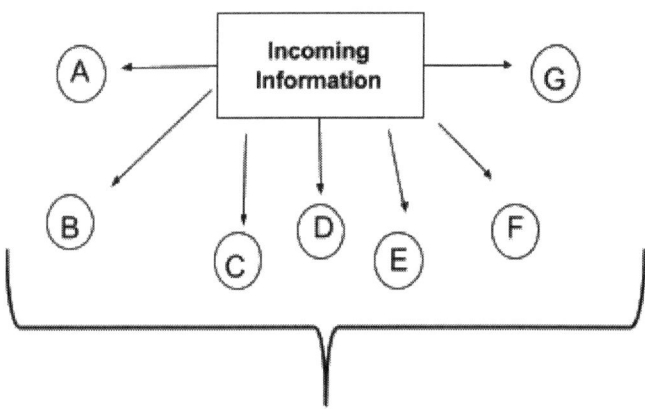

All the conclusions you can derive.

Things to try:

- The "plus, minus, interesting" technique.[26] Think of the positive, the negative, and what you find interesting in

---

[25] Hall, L M., and Bob G. Bodenhamer. *Mind-lines : lines for changing minds.* Clifton, CO: NSP, Neuro-Semantics Publications, 2005. Print.

[26] De, Bono E. *Six Thinking Hats.* Boston: Little, Brown, 1999. Print.

each situation. This lets you take on multiple perspectives and not get stuck on one way of seeing things.
- What would someone that knows plenty about this issue do? How would they think about it?
- 20 techniques to re-frame from *Mindlines* by Michael Hall.

Three different meanings

Things on their own, don't have meaning. You give meaning to them. The meaning you give to something will be different from others.

The advantage is that you can choose the meaning that most benefits you. Nelson Zink said, *"try giving every event at least three different meanings and see how this changes your world."*

Maybe you lose your job. You can see it as an opportunity to pursue the path you've been wanting to take. Now you have no excuses. You can see it as the end of the world, you're worthless and you will never, ever get another job. Maybe see it as a hit to your ego and self-esteem. Maybe you view it as a wakeup call that things need to change in your life, your work ethic, your time management, and people skills. Maybe getting fired was unjustified and you realized that it wasn't a place where you could grow and build a career. Maybe it's a sign you should try another field where your strengths can be put to better use.

You choose which meaning you give to whatever happens to you. Framing situations in different ways lets you reap more benefits.

How do you know for sure that losing your job means the end of the world? How would you know that's true or false? Does losing your job always mean the end of the world? Is there a possibility that losing your job may be an opportunity for a new beginning? If it's the end of the world, does it matter if you have a job or not?

If you had your job and hated it, would that be a good thing for you?

Things to try:

- Come up with three different perspectives for any situation or problem? Do it regularly. Look at it from different angles. Now what do you see?
- Think about the negative and positive situations in your life and find three different meanings for them.

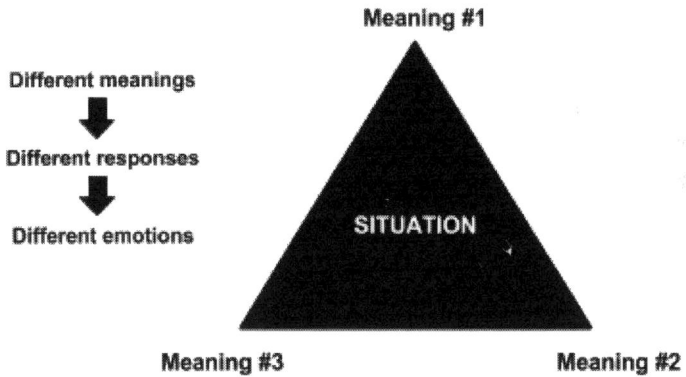

Zimbardo's time perspectives

Philip Zimbardo in his book, *The Time Paradox*,[27] discusses how the way we perceive psychological time, defines how we live and who we are. Psychological time is how we perceive the passing of time; the way we look at the past, present, future, and how it affects the way we live our lives. You can take the test on the website *www.thetimeparadox.com* to determine your time perspectives.

Past positive and past negative are the two ways we view past events in our lives. Events in our past or childhood, psychologists like Alfred Adler believed, would explain our present problems. How do you view your past? Is it full of good memories and positive experiences or do you have many regrets and painful memories?

A past positive attitude helps people be happier, healthier, and live better than those who view things in a past negative perspective. Even more surprising, if your understanding or memory of the past is not accurate, you'll still be better off than the past negative group. This time perspective allows you to view your past with gratitude and provides more fulfillment in the present.

---

[27] Zimbardo, Philip G., and John Boyd. *The time paradox : the new psychology of time that will change your life*. New York: Free Press, 2008. Print.

The present hedonist, focuses on the pleasure of living in the present and doesn't consider the future. The present fatalist believes that fate has already been decided and there is no point in worrying about the future. They believe it doesn't matter what they do, as they have no control over the future.

Future oriented people think further ahead. They plan ahead and consider the pros and cons of their decisions. They decide the present, based on what they desire for the future.

People have a mix of time perspectives, being weak in some and strong in others. The *Time Paradox* concludes that the best mix of time perspectives is:

- High in past positive
- Moderately high in present hedonist
- Moderately high in future orientation
- Low on past negative and present fatalist

Look at the past as positive and be grateful for it. Focus on the present moment and fully enjoy it. Adding in some future orientation helps you be hopeful for a better tomorrow and work in the present, to build the future you want.

To switch from past negative to past positive try the "Who was I" exercise from The Time Paradox:

- Ask yourself "Who was I" twenty times and write down different answers. Count how many are positive and how many are negative.

- Write down 3 negative events and what positive lessons you learned from them.
- Write down ways you can use those lessons to improve your future.
- Write down what you are grateful for every day.
- Repeat the *"Who was I"* exercise a few weeks later and determine if there are more positives than negatives.

To develop a present orientation try:

- Meditation
- Paying attention to the sounds, smells, and your surroundings
- Listen
- Pay attention to how you feel (use Plutchik's wheel) and determine why you feel that way.

To develop a future orientation try:

- Describing who you want to be and the life you want to have.
- Listing out the goals that will help you achieve this.
- Making a plan, setting a deadline, and getting to work.

QUESTIONS

- Do you have a present hedonist or present fatalist perspective?
- Do you have a hopeful view of the future?

- Do you think you will look back on current challenges in a negative way or will they be something you are grateful for?
- How will you view your present when it becomes your past? Will it be positive or negative?
- How will this situation influence your present and your future?
- How do you see your past? Can you learn some lessons and use them to build a better future?
- How can you change the way you look at your present to create a better future?

Long term vs. Short term thinking

Humans are short sighted. We tend to focus on what's directly in front. When you drive on the road what are you focused on? The car in front of you, the mirrors, the rearview mirror, the car to the side of you, the cars in front of the car in front of you? Are you anticipating what the car directly in front of you will do because you're noticing the cars farther ahead are hitting the brakes? Are you only looking at the car in front? If you only look at the car right in front, the amount of time available to respond, is reduced.

It took people time to accept the idea of the automobile. How would something like that replace the horse and wagon? Yet it happened. It has freed humans from what used to be the limits of our town and has allowed us to travel farther and faster.

It took some time, but cars became the main form of transportation. What happened afterwards, we did not foresee. Our dependence on oil to run the new technology. The fumes and pollution that we would produce and the environmental damage it causes. The amount of roads we would build, in order to connect different towns, cities, states, countries, and people. The displacement of animal and plant habitats. The amount of concrete and asphalt that would be used to build the infrastructure necessary, for a growing population, with a growing amount of cars. The wars that would occur due to oil. The amount of deaths that would come from car accidents.

Why didn't we see it coming? Why didn't we consider the consequences? Did we think of the short term benefits and forget to consider the long term consequences? Were we focused on the immediate payoff?

Howard Marks calls this, "second level thinking." [28]

Second, is the key word here.

Given a choice between A and B, most people will decide which is better based on the pros and cons.

The second level thinker will consider the consequences of choice A and they'll ask, and then what? What will happen as a result of that? What are the pros and cons of the consequences?

Then they'll do the same thing with choice B.

If you want to look further ahead at the consequences, go to the third level or the fourth level. The further you go, the more clearly you understand the results of going down that path.

The "And then what?" question is commonly used in economics, but as Warren Buffett says, *"it is useful to ask in any situation."* [29]

---

[28] Marks, Howard. *The most important thing : uncommon sense for the thoughtful investor.* New York: Columbia University Press, 2011. Print.

[29] Bevelin, Peter. *Seeking Wisdom: From Darwin to Munger.* Malmö: PCA Publications, 2013. Print.

If you stay on the first level, you'll get the same results as everyone else. If you use second level thinking, you'll separate yourself from the crowd.

The documentary, *Real Value*,[30] offers a great example. A shirt you liked was selling for a low price, so you bought it. We're able to grasp the difference in price because it's immediate. We know how much we're paying just by looking at the price and we'll feel it in our wallet. But what if we asked, why it's so cheap? Is this company hiring children to work at their factory in poor working conditions and under paying them? What type of material is this and will it last more than one wash? Do they dispose of waste properly or cut corners? The price may be low, but what is the long term price of buying their products? What about the social, ethical, and environmental impact of sponsoring a company like this? We don't think about it because we can't immediately grasp the effect it'll have.

As Dan Ariely states in the documentary, *"maybe you think organic food is unaffordable, but perhaps it is our values and priorities that are unaffordable."*

Short term thinking was more useful when we lived in caves, hunted and gathered our food, and protected our loved ones from predators and the elements. We no longer live under those circumstances. Food doesn't need to be hunted. Water is easily available for a large part of the population. We don't have

---

[30] "Real Value | Economics Documentary with Dan Ariely | Sustainability | Social Entrepreneurship." *YouTube*, 4 Mar. 2014, www.youtube.com/watch?v=ez3CWXQrgVo.

predators, unless we're exposed to them in a jungle, savannah or the open sea.

We need to think longer term. See further into the future and consider the consequences of our decisions. The more forward looking we are, the better prepared we'll be to handle different situations that occur.

Long term thinking helps put things in perspective. If we make all our decisions on short term thinking, then we focus only on the present. In order to move towards a desirable future, we have to look further ahead and ask the right questions.

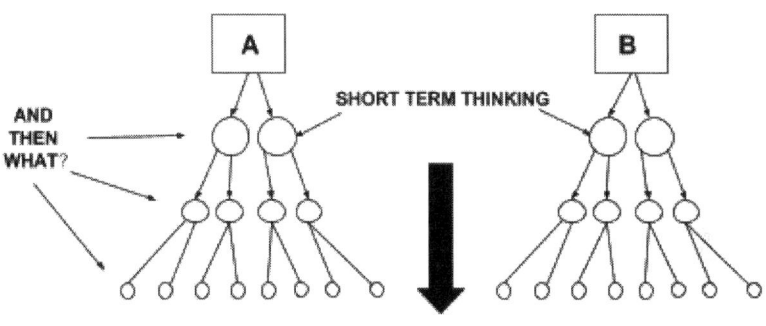

QUESTIONS

- And then what will happen?
- What will be the consequences of each option? What are the consequences of the consequences?
- What am I not seeing? What have I not considered?
- What can I learn here?

Cycles

Our lives are full of cycles. The cycle of day and night, the seasons, business and economic cycles, the water cycle. It's endless. Inside every day, your work, your relationships, your health, there are also cycles. Each part of the cycle brings different challenges and opportunities.

The economic cycle has four phases. In the expansion phase the market goes up and the economy grows. Then it begins to slow down and flattens out; it stops growing and enters the crisis phase. The amount of consumer spending goes down, companies begin to slow down their growth and start to cut back expenses. People begin to lose their jobs. The economy begins to enter the recession phase. In the recession, businesses close, unemployment rises, and people´s discretionary income decreases. As time passes, things begin to stabilize, turn around, and enter the recovery phase. Then the cycle begins again.

Expansion----> Crisis----> Recession ----> Recovery

When you're in the recovery and expansion phases, you don't have many worries. Yet, this is the best moment to prepare for the difficult times, which lie ahead. Prepare when things are easy, to profit from the hidden opportunities of crisis and recession phases. If you're unprepared, it'll be harder and you might not make it.

Consider the following, during the good times:

- Make a list of what you fear. What is the worst that could happen if what you fear occurs? How can you change your perspective and take advantage of it? Is this fear helping or hurting you?

- Are you playing to win or playing not to lose? When you're playing to win, you're open to the opportunities that arise from the challenges you face. When you play not to lose, you close yourself off to possibilities that can turn the situation around because you're afraid to take a risk. That doesn't mean you should take unmeasured risks. It means you have to weigh the costs and benefits and make sure the reward, is worth the risk. Playing to win will keep you open to the possibilities.

- Tune out the negative news. People will say it can't be done. What's important is where your focus is. Are you focused on what's possible or on all the things that can go wrong? If you've prepared, then you already have a plan for what can go wrong.

- Set big goals that'll challenge you and light a fire under your feet. Big goals require you to take massive action. They keep you busy. Lighting a fire under your feet means creating a sense of urgency. Doing what you can today and avoiding procrastination. Organizing your time so you are taking advantage of it and being as productive as possible, in order to get closer towards your goals.

- Adapt to the situation. Where in the cycle are you? Are you in an expansion phase, a recession, crisis or recovery phase? What can you do in each one to better set yourself up for success? How or what do you need to change to better position yourself?

- Accountability. Take responsibility for your actions. Where you are and what you do is on your shoulders.

- Look for the opportunities in the situation. Where are they? What are you missing? Who can provide alternate perspectives?

- Get rid of what doesn't work. When things are going well we don't pay attention to what is unnecessary. We pay attention to it, when we need to cut costs. In terms of your life, work, relationships, health, what do you need to get rid of because it doesn't add any value? What is not working and would allow you to reduce your costs quickly?

- Anticipate and prepare for future trouble. What are the things that will give you trouble and how can you prepare for them? What will you do if A happens? If B happens? If C happens? This way, when something different than expected happens, you are ready.

- Position yourself to explode after the difficult times. How can you take so much advantage of the difficult times that you actually end up ahead of where you were before? What situations can you place yourself in (short term) that will bring more benefits in the long term?

- Believe that your biggest challenges are your greatest teachers. If you pause to reflect on the most difficult moments in your life, what did you learn? What occurred as a result of going through that situation? It is the challenges we go through that allow us to learn the most and help us move to another level.

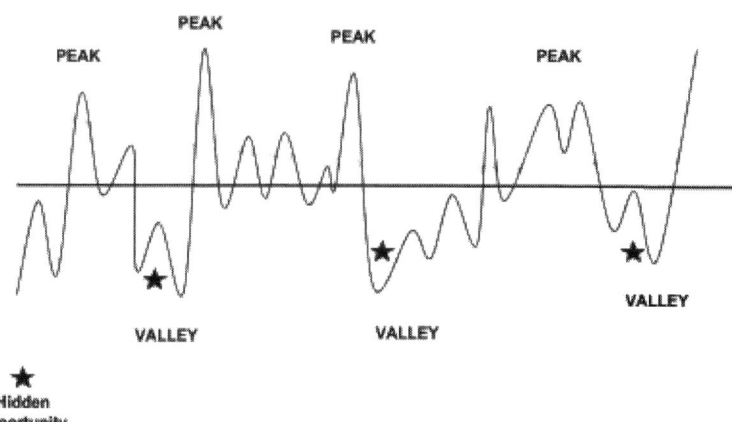

QUESTIONS

- If you think of your life in cycles, where would you consider yourself to be today, this week, this month, and

this year? If you are in a recession or crisis, what can you anticipate and plan for? What can you take advantage of?
- What part of the cycle is the economy in? Your business or job? Your relationship? Your health? Your financial situation?
- What can you do to maximize the benefits of each phase of the cycle? To reduce the risks and increase rewards?
- Where is your focus? Are you playing to win or playing not to lose?
- What are the biggest lessons you have learned from difficult times?
- How can you best set yourself up for explosive growth once the difficult part of the cycle ends?

The art of proving yourself wrong

Humans have a tendency to pay attention to ideas that support what they already believe. It's called the confirmation bias.

Charlie Munger, says that he "*never takes a stance on anything unless he can argue the other side better than the other person.*" That means he's looked at the issue from a variety of different perspectives and understands it well.

Have you been in a situation where you argued about something you believed in, but the opposing point of view, was a complete unknown to you? This lack of acceptance that other perspectives exist, keeps you from seeing other explanations and possibilities. It also prevents you from learning.

After developing his theory of evolution, Charles Darwin shared it only with a few close friends; he was afraid of how it would be received.[31] During this time, he thought about all the things that would be questioned and challenged in his work. Darwin searched for disconfirming evidence and then prepared responses and explanations for each one. It took Darwin over twenty years to finally release his theory to the public and by that time he was prepared for the criticism he'd receive.

---

[31] Richards, Robert J. "WHY DARWIN DELAYED, OR INTERESTING PROBLEMS AND MODELS IN THE HISTORY OF SCIENCE." Journal of the history of the behavioral sciences, 19 Jan. 1983, home.uchicago.edu/~rjr6/articles/Why%20Darwin%20Delayed.pdf.

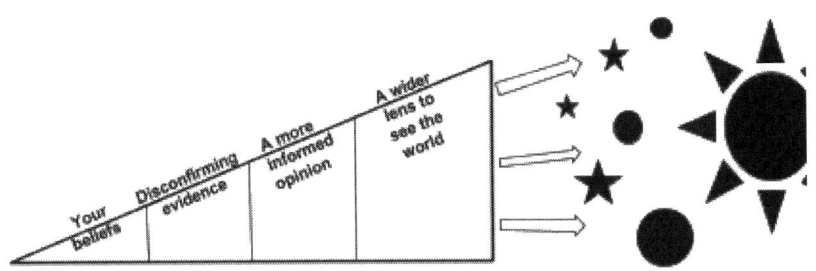

People who work in sales have scripts with responses to people's objections. This increases their chances of closing a sale. A good salesperson will be able to continue a conversation with a customer, despite all their objections, and eventually convince them to buy. They do this by preparing responses beforehand to all the possible objections. To understand what those objections are, you must consider other perspectives, especially those that disagree with yours.

Paul Arden puts this in an interesting way in, *It's right to be wrong*,

"*Start being wrong and suddenly anything is possible.*
You're no longer trying to be infallible.
You're in the unknown. There's no way of knowing what can happen, but there's more chance of it being amazing than if you try to be right.
Of course, being wrong is a risk...
Risks are a measure of people. People who won't take them are trying to preserve what they have. People who do take them often end up by having more.
Some risks have a future and some people call them wrong.

But being right may be like walking backwards proving where you've been." [32]

Things to try:

- Argue the other person's point of view. Try this when you're in a conflict.
- Come up with different perspectives, research evidence for them, and be able to argue them.
- Always consider the opposing viewpoint and study it. What can you learn from it? Does it help prove or disprove your beliefs? What did you learn that you didn't know before?
- Consider all the possible objections and then come up with responses for them.
- Learn from your enemies. Get their opinion. You may learn something about them, or yourself that you didn't know.
- Question everything you believe. Ask yourself why you believe that and what evidence you have. Is it true?
- Understand what people think and why they think that.
- Be curious and willing to challenge yourself. Be flexible in your thinking.
- Use Byron Katie´s questions: [33]

---

[32] Arden, Paul. *It's not how good you are, it's how good you want to be.* London New York: Phaidon, 2003. Print.

[33] Katie, Byron, and Stephen Mitchell. *Loving what is : four questions that can change your life.* New York: Harmony Books, 2002. Print.

1- Is it true?
2- Can you know that it is absolutely true?
3- How do you react when you think this way?
4- What would life be like, if you didn't have this thought?

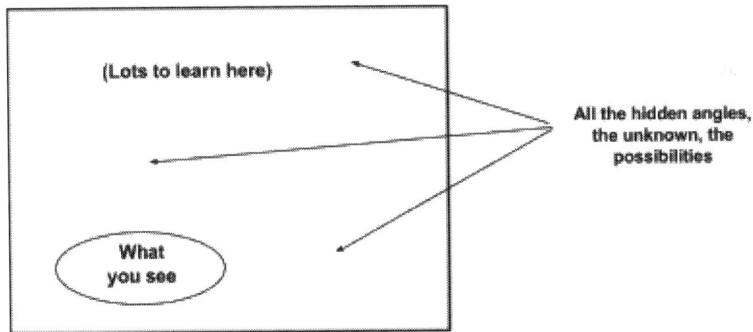

Part 4 - STRATEGIES TO COPE WITH LIFE'S CHALLENGES AND BUILD RESILIENCE

Deconstruct Things

Breaking things down into smaller pieces makes them much easier to work on. John Maxwell says that, "*hard things are the result of a bunch of easy things you didn't do when you should have.*" When you take it apart though, you'll see that it's possible. You just need to do it piece by piece. Brick by brick. That is how the wall is built.

Each part belongs to a greater whole. The greater whole is part of something even larger. Each part is also composed of smaller pieces.

Things to try:

- Deconstruct events, decisions, and challenges in your life. Then ask the following questions.

QUESTIONS

- What are the parts that add up to make the whole?
- How can you break this down to make it more simple or easy?
- How are the parts held together?
- What is the function of different parts and how important are they?
- Which parts have the most important functions? Could I focus on those?

- Would the whole still function without some parts? How well and why?
- Can you break it down even further?

DECONSTRUCT

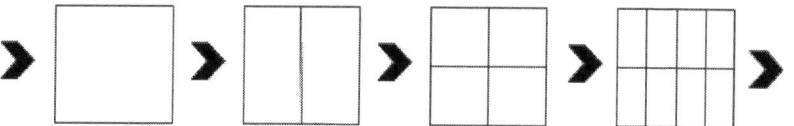

Adapting to the circumstances

A difference between experienced and young athletes, is the ability to adapt their goals, to the situation.

Mountain biker, Catharine Pendrel, tells the story of her participation in the Rio Olympics.[34] She had prepared for all the different types of scenarios. At least she thought so. Her goal was to give her best and race in a way she could be proud of. She wasn't focused on medals or trophies. What Pendrel didn't plan for, was the crash right at the beginning of the race that would mess up her bike's gear shift. Despite the problem, she got up and kept pedaling. She then had another crash. Once she reached her mechanic, Pendrel was in 25th place.

The mechanic quickly fixed the bike's gear shift and got her on her way. Luckily, Pendrel hadn't given up hope. When she reached the top of one of the hills, she realized she wasn't too far behind. Pendrel remembered that she had been in a similar situation before and was able to recover. Pendrel then focused on passing the biker right in front of her. Once she did that, she focused on passing the next biker. One by one, she overtook them until eventually, moving up to third place. She then fell again. Another test to her character, Pendrel got back up, kept her pace, and still managed to come in third and win bronze.

---

[34] Bercovici, Jeff. *Play on : the new science of elite performance at any age.* Boston: Houghton Mifflin Harcourt, 2018. Print.

Pendrel was able to adjust her goals to the current situation. She adapted. She was flexible. She was also not thrown off track because her goal wasn't a perfect race. It was simply to give her best and she did just that.

We set up our goals in a way that we can't control by focusing on external things. When we fail to achieve them, we get frustrated. Detach yourself from a particular way of things unfolding and stay flexible. Establish goals that focus on what you can control. Try setting a goal to keep an optimistic attitude and give your best effort, no matter what happens. You may be surprised by the result.

One reason we don't adapt well is that we get complacent. Because we're complacent we don't plan ahead and we don't notice that we have to adjust to new circumstances. We think that what works for us now and what we already know, will always work. We forget that life has cycles. Sometimes things work well and other times, nothing seems to work. Expect things to stop working.

We don't reflect on what's happening either. If we don't consider what's occurring, we won't notice that change is necessary and won't know how to adjust. We have to constantly be learning and developing our skills. If we don't do this, we won't know how to adapt, even when we know it's necessary.

Things to try:

- You have to recognize that there is a need to adapt. Let go of any feelings of complacency. Be uncomfortable. Be proactive in reading and staying on top of what's going on in the world. Consistently learn in order to be better prepared for the future and better set yourself up to win. Imagine it is 100 years into the future and ask yourself if this particular information is going to be meaningful and how.

- Do you see a problem? What can go wrong? Where is the next risk? Where are the opportunities in this situation? Ask yourself what is missing? What is not happening?

- Understand how you need to adapt. Research how people are adapting successfully to changes and how they are not. Is there anyone that has already had to go through this? Be open to new, different and better ideas of how to adapt. Stay curious and look for disconfirming evidence for your beliefs. Consider the consequences of what you think and do. Create a plan with a variety of scenarios. Leave room for the unknowns.

- Take the action necessary for adaptation. Observe what happens, ask for feedback, and adjust your actions if what you expect doesn't happen. Then repeat the process.

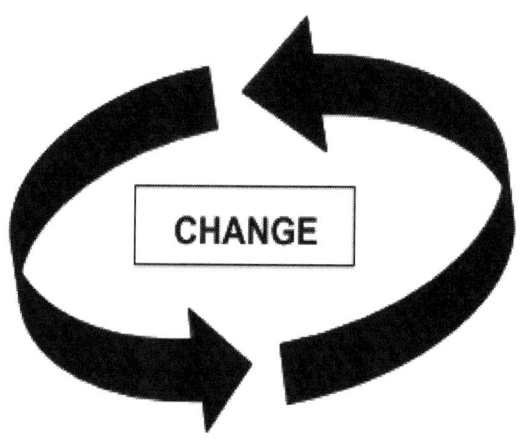

QUESTIONS

- What could happen in the near future?
- Where may things go wrong? Who has gone through this and can I learn from their experience, mistakes, and triumphs?
- Can you learn something from history to prepare in advance for this situation?
- What is changing and what is not changing? How will this affect you, your situation? How could you adjust to different scenarios?

Self talk

The difference between winners and losers is how they speak to themselves. You've heard it before, the little voice in your head that has an opinion on everything. The one that just won't shut up. That little voice that goes on and on randomly talking about different topics and having conversations with you and other people. The little voice is often focused on the negative instead of the positive. It looks for problems, instead of solutions.

There is a Native American parable of two wolves who battle every day inside each of us.[35] One wolf is evil. He's envious, angry, greedy, arrogant and resentful. The other wolf is good and represents love, peace, joy, hope and truth.

In the end, which wolf wins?

The one you feed.

The little voice in your head needs to be silenced, not fed.

Start by listening to what it's saying. Become an observer of the voice. When you do this, you'll detach from it. You'll notice you're not the voice. Then you'll be able to move forward without it distracting you.

---

[35] "Cherokee Legend - Two Wolves." *First People of America - The Native Americans A.k.a. American Indians*, www.firstpeople.us/FP-Html-Legends/TwoWolves-Cherokee.html.

Things to try:

- Set an alarm to ring every 30 minutes as a reminder to be mindful and focused on the task at hand. Be present. If you catch yourself paying attention to useless thoughts, refocus your mind.
- You can also choose to use positive affirmations that help shift your focus to where you want, in order to achieve your goal. By doing this you are controlling what is being said, in your head.
- Pretend you're a coach and talk to yourself from that perspective. Think of how a high level coach would talk to you in different situations. Let them encourage you and provide useful feedback. By assuming different points of view, you'll see things in different ways.
- Practice mindfulness meditation and breathing. Be focused on the moment and on what you're doing.

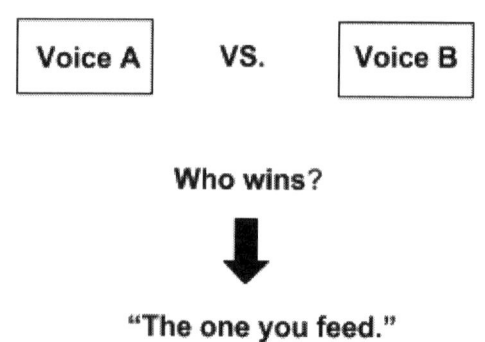

QUESTIONS

- What kind of things does the little voice in your head say? Are they helpful or are they hurting you?
- Are you present and focused on what you're doing or is your body in one place and your head in another? How can you bring them together?
- Do you talk to yourself like a supportive coach or are you the type of coach that just criticizes and puts down?

Optimism

Martin Seligman, in his book, *Learned Optimism*, shows why it's useful to approach life with optimism.[36]

- Optimists consider problems as temporary.
- Optimists view problems specific to a situation.
- Optimists view negative events as the result of external circumstances and positive events as the result of internal causes.
- Optimists are healthier and have stronger immune systems.
- Optimists are more likely to stick to their plan and work towards their goals because they believe they're in control of their life.
- Optimists have less negative life experiences and less stress.
- Optimists have stronger friendships so they have people to lean on, when times get tough.
- Optimists tend to be happier people.
- Optimists are better at handling rejection.

Whatever you do, being optimistic is useful.

---

[36] Seligman, Martin E. *Learned optimism*. New York: A.A. Knopf, 1991. Print.

The opposite of optimism is pessimism. Somewhere in between is realism. They all have something to teach us. When you are pessimistic about something, it's useful to question why that is. What's going on that is making you pessimistic and how can you change it? What needs to happen in order to be optimistic?

It also helps to be realistic. Hold yourself accountable, ask for objective feedback and measure your progress. By doing this, you'll stay grounded in reality and avoid wishful thinking.

Things to try:

'Seligman's ABC TECHNIQUE'

- *Adversity*- Think of a challenging situation in your life.

- *Belief*- How do you interpret this situation?

- *Consequences*- How do you respond as a result of the 'Adversity' and 'Belief'?

***Pay attention to the ABC's in your life. Question your beliefs and have a trusted friend do so, as well.

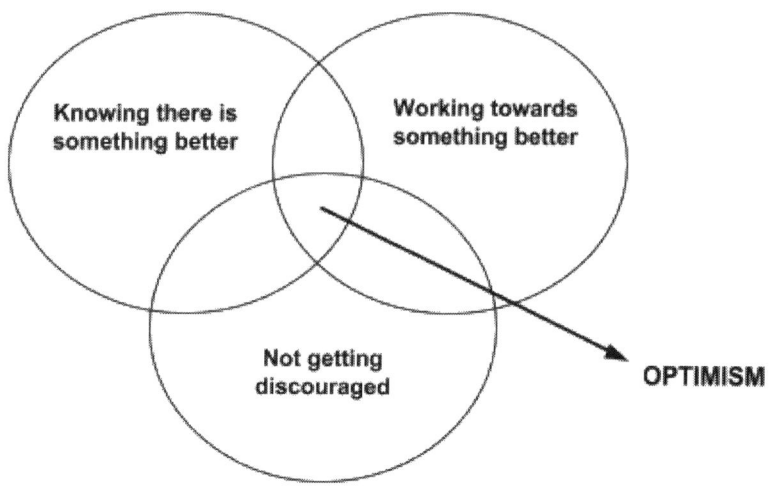

QUESTIONS

- Is this actually true?
- Is there another explanation?
- If it were true, what would it mean for me?
- Is it helpful\ useful to think this way?
- What if you switched what you thought about something? Instead of seeing it as stressful or uncomfortable, think of it as exciting and fun. What benefit could that bring? What benefit is there in seeing it in a negative way?
- What about this situation are you optimistic about? Pessimistic about? Realistic about? How might you be able to switch your point of view in these areas? What would you need to do for that to happen?

Frustration + Curiosity = Progress

Frustration is a reaction to problems that we don't yet know how to solve. It happens when we feel we're not getting anywhere, when others don't do what we want or act the way we want. When we feel we have no control over a situation. It arises from uncertainty and inability to do something about things within and outside our control. It can also come from conflicting desires.

There are two types of frustration; internal which you can change and external which you can't do much about. When you get frustrated, be curious and ask what's causing you to feel that way. Is the root of the frustration internal or external? Your curiosity will help you understand the issue and think of ways to resolve it. If you try to ignore the frustration, it can lead to anger, annoyance, stress, depression, less confidence, and aggression.[37]

Things to try when feeling frustrated:

- Talk to someone about it
- Spend time with supportive people
- Consider different ways to solve the problem. What do you need to learn so you can move forward?

---

[37] Berger, Vincent F. "Frustration." *Psychologist Anywhere Anytime*, www.psychologistanywhereanytime.com/emotional_problems_psychologist/pyschologist_frustration.htm.

- Ask yourself, "on a scale from 1-5, how big of a problem is this?
- Can you do anything about it? If yes, take the necessary action. If no, practice patience and look for other possible solutions.
- Focus on your breathing
- Meditate
- Take a break and do something fun and relaxing
- Exercise

Whatever you're feeling, transmits energy that other people pick up on. Those feelings influence how you act, how you perceive everything that happens to you, and that creates a ripple effect in all areas of your life.

See frustration as another challenge you have to go through, to get where you want. Once you overcome it, you'll have learned something new and you'll be better able to handle the next set of problems.

QUESTIONS

- Do you avoid digging into your frustration? How does that usually work out?
- Why are you frustrated? Where is it coming from?
- Is it internal or external frustration?
- What can I do to solve this issue? Can you substitute it with another feeling?
- What can help you take your mind off of this?
- Have you tried to reframe the frustration?
- Who can you talk to?

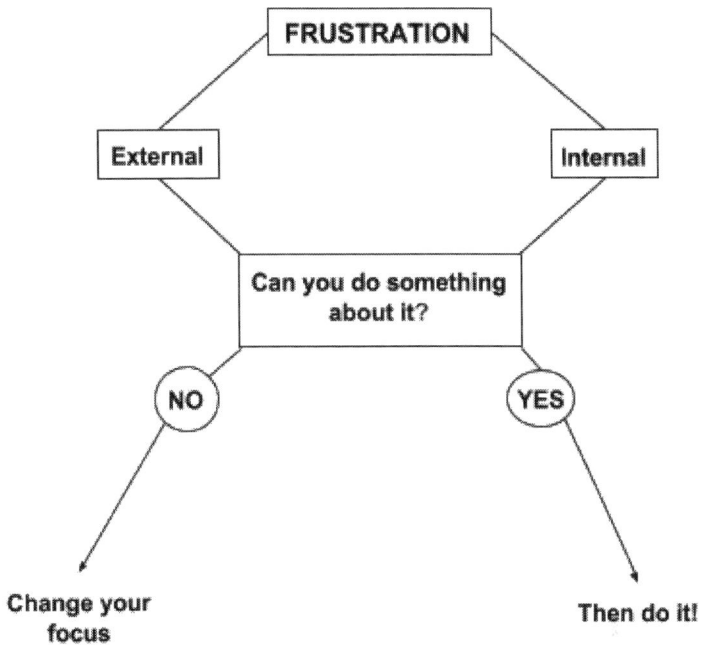

Solution focused thinking leads to possibilities

When faced with problems, our default mode leads us to focus on the problem, why it occurred to us, and the consequences. When we dwell on a problem for a long time, we create a domino effect of negativity.

Instead of focusing on the problem, work on coming up with possible solutions. Be resourceful! How can you get out of this situation? What steps could you take to make things better? Who can you ask for help?

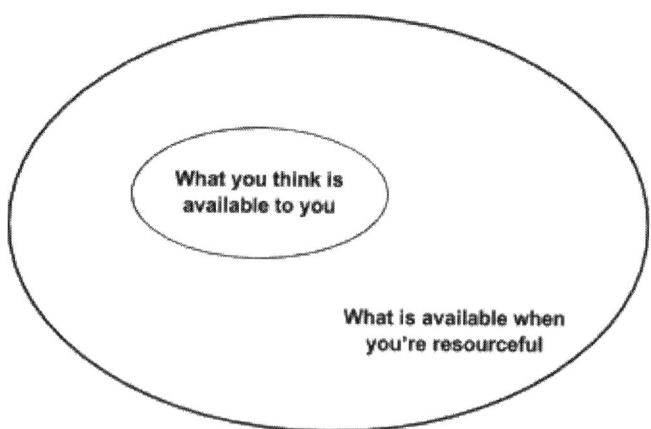

No matter how much you think you know about a situation, there'll always be things you can't see. There are always unknowns. If you let that stop you from taking action, you'll never do anything. It doesn't matter if it's not the right move or the perfect solution. Your first move may not be the best. But you'll be smart enough to know when one solution isn't working and can move on to the next one. Even the wrong move will provide insight on the right direction.

As General George Patton said, "*a good plan, violently executed now, is better than a perfect plan next week.*"

Get moving. Stop thinking about it endlessly. Get the information you need and then act. Situations and plans and people change. Accept that it will happen and build plans along the way for those situations.

When you're focused on solutions, you'll move from worrying about problems to conquering them.

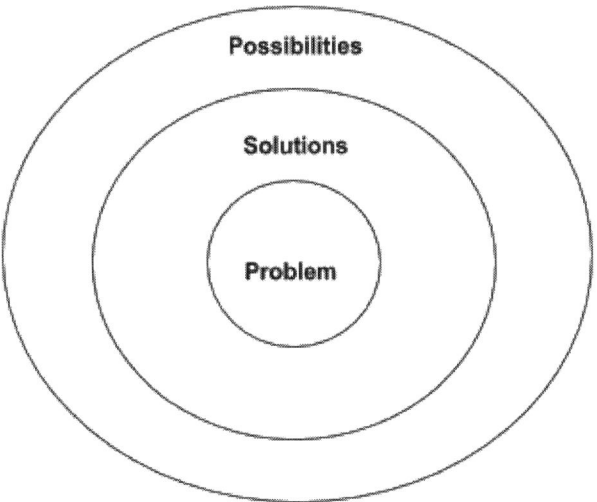

Things to try:

- Look for solutions. Consider what you can do with what you have. Be resourceful!
- Stay open minded and determine what is and what is not possible.
- Develop your curiosity and imagination. Constantly learn and research and put it into action. Make new connections.
- Be proactive. Believe that it is possible and work to create the circumstances necessary.
- Be a giver. The more you help others, the easier it will be for you to get help when you need it.
- Look at those who have already done it and stand on their shoulders.
- Ask for help.
- Improvise. Break the rules.
- Try different options.
- Trust and encourage others to focus on solutions, rather than problems.

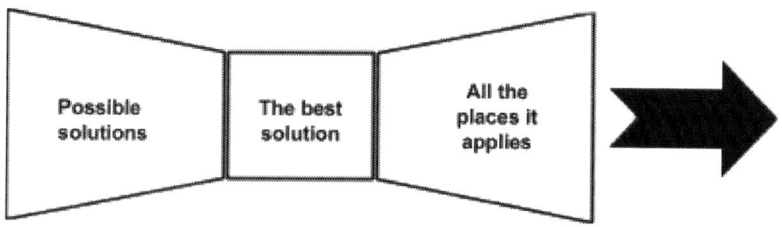

QUESTIONS

- Are you focused on the problem or solutions? What are all the possible solutions you can think of?
- If you don't have the knowledge, who can help? How can you connect with these people?
- Is there anyone that has already gone through this and can you learn from what they did?
- How can you do more with what you have, with who you know, and where you're at?
- How resourceful are you?
- If you were more resourceful, how would your life be different?
- What's one thing I can do right now to make this situation better?

Accountability

We have a higher chance of accomplishing our goals, if we're held accountable. We can do it ourselves or we can have someone else hold us accountable. Accountability forces us to stay true to ourselves and what we're actually doing. It makes us look in the mirror, be objective, and prevents us from lying to ourselves. Accountability also keeps us responsible for our actions and rids us of the victim mentality. Let go of excuses and complaints. Look for explanations instead. Excuses are a way to avoid taking responsibility. It takes character to be honest, admit you messed up, and tell the truth. Take responsibility for your actions.

It's not what we think about doing or the intention, but what we do, that counts. Regardless of the results. Even if what you do ends up being a horrible idea or yielding an undesirable result, you learn from it and try again.

You will try. You will mess up and fail. You will learn. You will try again. You will do better.

Things to try:

- Perform the tasks you said you would.
- Be reliable and trustworthy.
- One way to make this change is to create experiences that create the new beliefs you want.
- Stop blaming others and taking the role of the victim. You get to decide how you respond.

- Ask for feedback so you can better see what you cannot see about yourself.
- Own up to the situation.
- Pick the right people to hold you accountable.
- See the problem----> accept the problem--> come up with solutions---> change it----> continue until next problem arises and then repeat process.
- Give a friend a large amount of money and have them donate it to a charity if you don't keep your word.

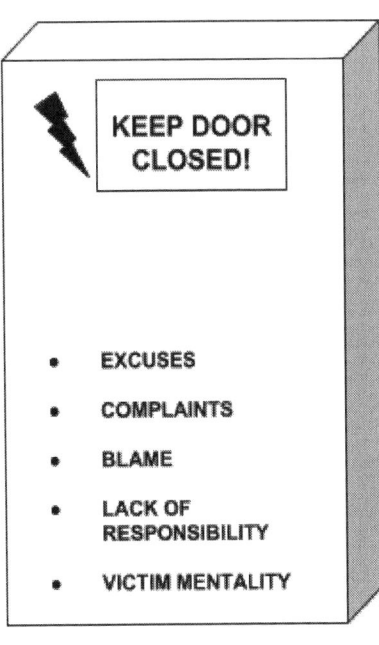
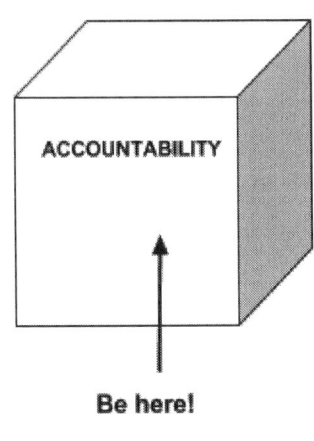

QUESTIONS

- Are you being accountable? Who holds you accountable for what you do and say?
- Is this an excuse or an explanation? Is it the honest truth?
- Are you complaining? Can you list all the benefits versus the negatives in this situation? Compare the lists. In a week, month, year from now, what will be more useful to me?
- Are you acting like a victim? What is something you can do right now to get out of the victim mentality and resolve the issue?
- What are some possible solutions?

Not taking it personally

You don't know what other people are going through. You may think you know, but unless they're very open about it, chances are you don't. They may be having a hard time dealing with difficult circumstances in their life. That may affect how they treat you. Whatever happens, don't take it personally. If you do, you'll end up feeling pain and hurt. It's better to just let it go.

The second agreement in, *The four agreements*, by Don Miguel Ruiz, is to *"never take anything personally."*[38] When we take something personally we're showing that we agree with what someone else is saying about us. You're the only one that can know if what they believe or say about you, is true. If you get offended and let it bother you, you're in a way, agreeing with their judgement.

It is often a projection of their inner feelings, their own fears, or a situation they're going through.

There's a lot to learn from what other people say about you. There's also truth to what they say and there are certain flaws you hadn't noticed. Your enemies can make you aware of where you're weak. What others say to you also tells you about the other person and can help to clarify, who they really are.

---

[38] Ruiz, Miguel. *The four agreements : a practical guide to personal freedom*. San Rafael, Calif: Amber-Allen Pub. Carlsbad, Calif. Distributed by Hay House, Inc, 1997. Print.

Instead of taking things personally, be open and get as much as you can from what others say to you. That may mean distancing yourself from some people. It may also mean taking a good, honest look at yourself and making some changes.

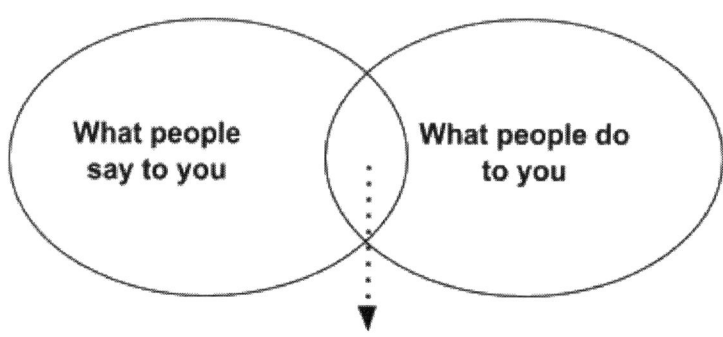

Something to learn about them and about yourself

QUESTIONS

- Is what this person saying about you true? Do they sincerely mean it? Is it something you agree with?
- If you don't agree, do you need to pay attention to them? If you do agree with them, what can you do to improve this? Can you thank them for the info and move on? Does it require more discussion? Is there a point to doing that at all?
- Is there anything you can learn about them through what they say? What can you learn about yourself?
- What benefit is there to taking this personally?

Feedback & measuring progress

> *"The chances of impacting performance increase with frequency and timeliness of feedback. That implies the need for ongoing, "how are we doing conversations. It's our best chance of knowing whether we're on track or not."*
>
> —Steve Roesler [39]

Top level performers are not affected by criticism in a negative way. They actively seek out constructive criticism from people they respect and use it to improve their performance. Lower level performers get upset, emotional and take things personally. The top performers use it as fuel to get better and better.

It's more useful to seek criticism, than praise.

It is hard to know if you're getting good at something, if you don't step back and look at things from an objective perspective. It's not only your opinion you should pay attention to. Sometimes you're too close to the action and develop a biased point of view.

Great athletes and musicians record their performances to use them as feedback in measuring progress. A recorder is a mirror to the musician, while a camera is a mirror to a tennis player.

---

[39] Roesler, Steve. "What, Why and How: Feedback." *All Things Workplace*, www.allthingsworkplace.com.

Recordings provide a realistic, unbiased perspective that show the performers flaws and strengths.

Coaches, mentors and people who have the skills you desire and whom you respect, can provide constructive criticism and feedback. Keep in mind that what they say, is only one person's opinion. Ideally, try to ask more people. Get lots of feedback. You'll be exposed to different points of view, see things you hadn't noticed, and have more ideas of how to move to the next level.

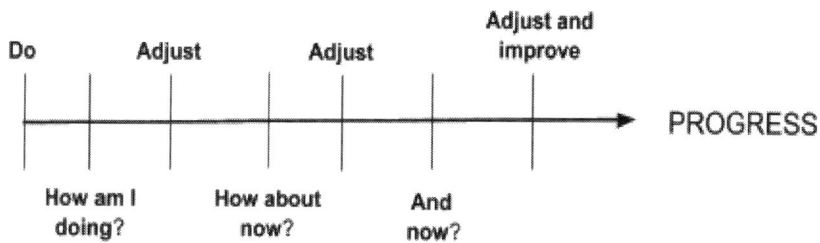

Things to try:

- Be able to distinguish between constructive criticism and destructive criticism.
- Consider whose feedback you value most and why. Do these people matter?
- According to Mark McGuinness, *"Good criticism has perspective, is specific, provides examples, is relevant and respectful."* [40]

---

[40] McGuinness, Mark. *Resilience: Facing Down Rejection & Criticism on the Road to Success.*, 2013. Print.

- Distance yourself from your work. Use space, time and other people's perspective. Use a camera, a recorder, another person.
- Review your work and performance.
- Choose what you will measure and keep track of. Compare yourself to your prior performance. Compare yourself to who you were yesterday, a week ago, and a month ago.

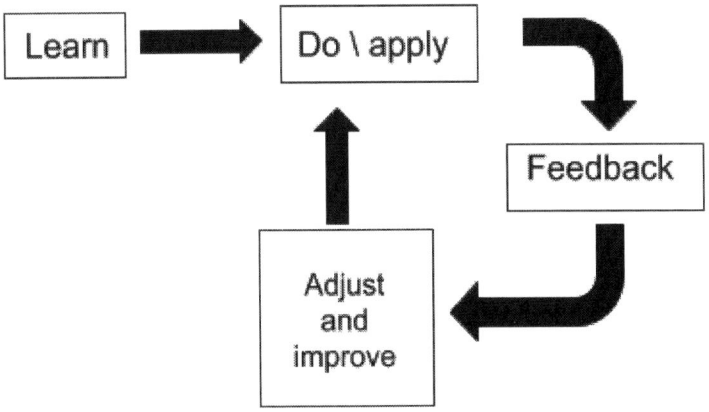

QUESTIONS

- What did you do well? What needs to improve? How can you improve this? Score it from 1-10 in different areas? How can you make it a 10?
- Go over your performance. Watch the video, hear the recording, look at the work and take it apart. Edit and improve constantly.
- How will you measure your progress?

- Will keeping track of your current actions move you toward your goal? What do you need to do daily to get to the end goal?
- Is it the end result that's important to you or the process? Where are you going to spend most of your time? If you are a constant work in progress, is your focus in the right place?

Compete

Place yourself in situations where you test your ability and skill level. It commonly happens in business, sports, music, and you can find ways to compete in other areas as well.

Josh Waitzkin, in an interview with Tim Ferriss,[41] talks about fighting the dirtiest opponents. By doing this he would put himself in situations which would test him in different ways. The dirty players would take cheap shots to try and get him to lose control. By learning to respond in a non-obvious way, he was able to control his opponent and not be surprised by the unexpected.

Waitzkin also says, "It's very interesting to observe who the top competitors pick out when they're five rounds into the sparring sessions and they're completely gassed. The ones who are on the steepest growth curve look for the hardest guy there—the one who might beat them up—while others look for someone they can take a break on."

Things to try:

- Get a sparring partner to compete with and test yourself. Aim for different ability levels. Someone better, someone at the same level, and someone at a lower level.

---

[41] Ferriss, Tim. "Becoming the Best Version of You." *The Blog of Author Tim Ferriss*, 25 Sept. 2017, tim.blog/2016/12/20/becoming-the-best-version-of-you/.

- Measure your improvement by comparing where you were yesterday, last week, last month, with where you are *today*.

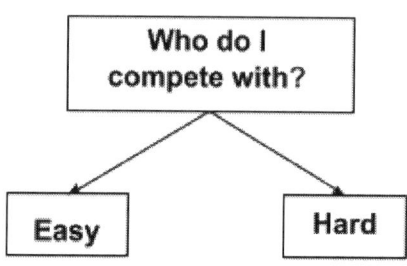

**What will bring
me the most benefit?**

QUESTIONS

- Are you getting better over time?
- Where are your weak spots and strong points? What do you need to work on?
- Who can you get as a sparring partner so you can practice what you're learning?
- What can you do to place yourself in situations that force you to compete in different areas of your life?
- Who are the people you look up to and why? What qualities do they possess that you admire?
- How can you set a new personal best? What will you need to do in order to keep challenging yourself?
- How can you turn this into a game and compete with yourself, get better, keep improving?

Be okay looking foolish

> *"If a person gave away your body to some passerby, you'd be furious. Yet you hand over your mind to anyone who comes along, so they may abuse you, leaving it disturbed and troubled – have you no shame in that?"*
>
> – Epictetus

We care too much about the way we look, when doing something. When we value other people's opinions of us more than ours, we limit ourselves. We make decisions based on what's accepted by others and by what's expected of us. In this process, we forget what's important to us; placing more importance in fitting in, rather than standing out. As the Japanese proverb goes, *"the nail that stands, gets hammered down."* No matter what you do and how well you do it, someone is going to hammer you down. Take the risk anyway.

When you start something new, you'll need to learn many skills before you are competent. When you first begin to ride your bike without training wheels, you lose balance and fall. The first time you kick a football, you may kick the ground or trip. Your legs and feet aren't used to the motion. The first time you talk in public, your voice may crack and you may sweat like crazy. It happens to everyone. But through practice, you get better at it and it becomes second nature.

Things to try:

- Be a beginner and try many new things.
- Empty your cup and forget all you think you know.

- Be a fool.
- Stop caring so much what others will think. You have no control over it.

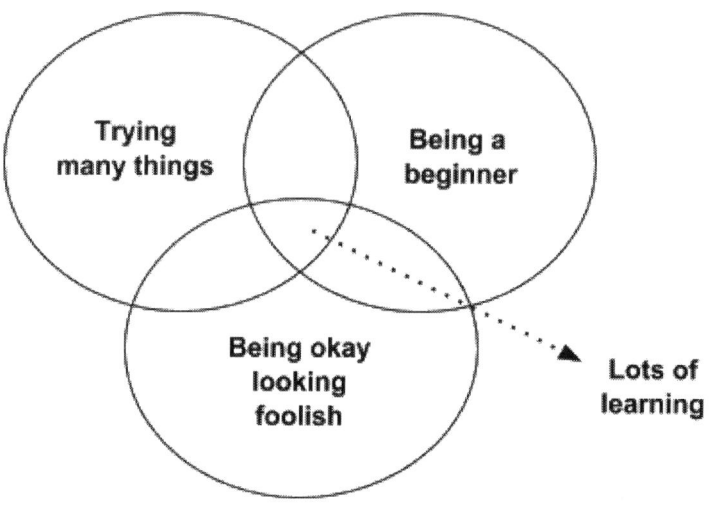

QUESTIONS

- Are you trying to avoid looking like a fool? Is there any benefit to that? Is there more pain in looking like a fool or being a fool because you don't take a chance?
- Is looking like a fool within your control or outside of it? If it's outside your control, then why does it bother you?
- What is the worst that could happen?
- Are you willing to look like a fool in order to get really good at something?

What would *'they'* do?

You're in a restaurant, see an attractive woman, but you don't know what to do. Who's someone you know that is great at talking to women? Who's not good at it? James Bond seems to know what he's doing. Mr. Bean would be the opposite.

- Ask yourself what would James Bond do? What would he not do?
- What would Mr. Bean do? What would Mr. Bean not do?

These questions all provide different ideas. Some better than others. While James Bond will provide a model to imitate, Mr. Bean, on the surface, shows what to avoid. Mr. Bean however, knows how to use humor. Since people enjoy laughing, he may look to approach by doing or saying something funny. That's one way you could start a conversation.

While certain actions work for these characters, they may not work for you. What are your strengths? When you figure that out, you can use them in your favor.

One size doesn't fit all. You could approach a woman with a big, friendly smile, but if you don't like the way your teeth look and don't like smiling, you'll look awkward. Maybe you're funny and can make people laugh. Humor is going to work better for you.

There is no single approach that always works. There is the approach that works for you. To know what that is, you have to test, observe and practice.

Things to try:

- Apply this same concept to your business and to different areas of your life.

QUESTIONS

- In your business, you could ask what Amazon, Facebook, Netflix, Wikipedia, Google, or Walmart would do?
- How would they run this business? What would they change\ improve?
- How would someone who's fit and healthy, eat? What would their diet look like? Exercise routine?
- How would a successful person manage their day and their time?
- How does a good leader motivate and inspire their team?
- Think of specific people and companies and study them. Read everything you can about them and you'll be better able to answer these questions in detail. Then take action.

These questions provide ideas and perspectives that you haven't considered. They can spark innovation. Invert the questions and ask what they would not do? What would they avoid?

Gratitude and enthusiasm

"When you arise in the morning, think of what a precious privilege it is to be alive - to breathe, to think, to enjoy, to love."

-Marcus Aurelius

Make a list of everything in your life you're grateful for. Write it out in a notebook, your phone or a piece of paper that you carry in your wallet. Every morning when you wake up, take a look at it, read it, and think about those things. Consider what life would be like, without them.

Perhaps you're thankful that you have all your limbs and are able to use them. Think about how your life would change if you didn't. Maybe you're thankful for having your parents around and being able to spend time with them. What would it be like without them?

Maybe it's being able to breathe oxygen without the help of an oxygen tank? Maybe it's your work, your health, a family member, music, your children, your spouse, your home, clothes, a warm bed, the food in the fridge.

Being grateful makes you focus on what you do have. We often focus on what we don't have and what we still haven't obtained, despite our effort. Instead, try following Jim Rohn's advice and, *"learn to be happy with what you have, while you pursue what you want."*

Considering what life would be like, without the things you're grateful for, is a form of negative visualization. When we think of losing something, we value it more. When you're feeling angry or your mind starts feeding the negative side of you, refocus your thinking and consider what you're grateful for. You can use the list you made or you can simply try and find what you're grateful for in that situation.

If you're stuck in bumper to bumper traffic, for example, you can be grateful that you have a car and are able to drive to any place you'd like. You have the freedom to travel and aren't limited to public transportation. You choose who travels with you and can offer a ride to a friend or family member. You can afford to pay for gas. You have space, you're comfortable, and are able to sit down, while others stand on the bus or train. You decide if you want the windows down, the AC on, or the heater. You determine what music plays on the radio. You choose how fast, slow, and safe you drive.

No matter the situation, try to find something to be grateful for.

Norman Vincent Peale shares some ideas in, *Enthusiasm makes the difference*,[42] to keep us grateful, enthusiastic, and excited:

- Have goals, a larger purpose, and some type of objective that makes you excited to get up in the morning. When was the last time you jumped out of bed, excited to start the day? What would it take to make that happen?

---

[42] Peale, Norman V. *Enthusiasm makes the difference*. Kingswood: World's Work, 1973. Print.

- At the end of each day, take all the things that are worrying you, causing you pain or suffering or that bother you and bring them together. Then release them. It takes time to get it to work, but after some practice it will help you in letting go.

- Think of all the good things you know before you get out of bed.

- Keep your mind renewed and excited. Learn new things, read great stories, feed your mind, meet and talk with great people, get inspired.

- Walking is often prescribed to people who suffer from depression. It allows the mind to disconnect from thoughts and focus more on the physical movement. Not strolling but walking faster than your normal pace. It allows you to rid yourself of worry and the physical activity releases endorphins and makes you feel better.

- Volunteer- Find causes you feel strongly about and volunteer your time. Spend some time in an orphanage, old folks home, in a hospital, with terminally ill patients, with refugees, etc. Talk with people, listen to them, and learn from them. It helps to support them and it will help you to put your life into perspective.

- Every day is a new day. Something different is happening, things you didn't know, others that you did, but have now changed. Problems have come up here and there, some small, some big. Accept that each day will be different, unpredictable, and uncertain. That's part of what makes life interesting, fun, a cycle of ups and downs. Once you accept that, you're going to be better prepared to handle things that come your way.

- Look for a reason to be grateful in every negative situation or uncomfortable moment.

- Write thank you notes to people who have given you something (friendship, a gift, a kind word, their time, etc.)

Complaints	What I'm thankful for...
{ Leave blank }	{ Fill this in }

QUESTIONS

- What are you grateful for in your life?
- List all the difficult situations you can think of and write out all the things you could be grateful for in each one.
- What are day to day situations that bother you? How could you be grateful for them?
- What is exciting about this? What isn't exciting and how could you change it? What would make you more enthusiastic about this?
- How could you be a more enthusiastic person? What could that do for your relationships, outlook on life, career, and family?
- What one thing could you start doing today to be more enthusiastic from the moment you get up?

What you've overcome

Write down all the obstacles and difficult situations you've gone through in your life and overcome. When you feel discouraged or frustrated, go through the list and take a look at where you are today. We tend to pay attention to what causes us pain and hurt.

When we realize the difficulties we've overcome in the past, we see how resilient we are. Life will bring challenges and problems our way. This no longer surprises us. We've been there before and we'll be able to get through it again.

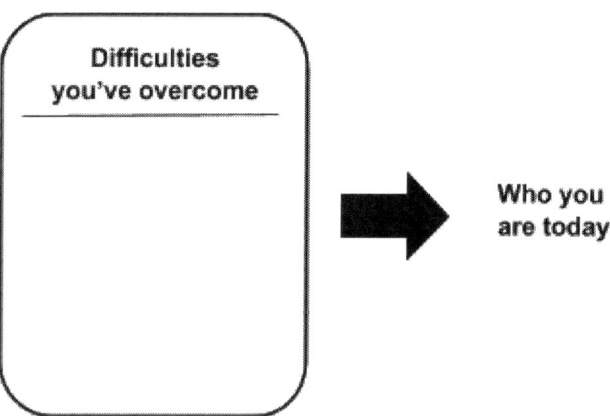

QUESTIONS

- What have you tried that was hard, but were able to overcome? What frustrations and difficulties have you survived that have made you stronger as a result?
- What new situations will you add to this list this year?

Find the humor, laugh, have fun, and play

"A day without laughter is a day wasted."

-Charlie Chaplin

Laughter, smiling and having fun have many benefits.

- Laughter lets people deal with stressful or frightening situations in a better way.
- Making patients in a hospital laugh takes their focus away from their health issues and the medical treatment.
- In studies, [43] laughter was shown to improve the patient's response to medical treatment.
- Laughter improves our mood and psychological well being.
- Laughter distracts us from getting stuck in negative thoughts and lets us better cope with depression.
- Humor enables us to find the funny in different situations we go through and not take ourselves too seriously.
- Smiling in front of the mirror for a set amount of time is used as treatment for patients with depression.
- Smiling often makes you appear friendlier and open when communicating with others.

---

[43] Earleywine, Mitchell. *Humor 101*. New York: Springer, 2011. Print.

- Laughter and play releases endorphins which make us feel better.

The older you get, the more you forget how fun it was to play games. Could it be a good way to spend our time as an adult? Games provide benefits to our productivity, creativity, and relationships says Jane McGonigal in, *Reality is broken*.[44] People who play video games develop their ability to collaborate and work in a team. They are better able to determine other people's strengths and weaknesses. They know the right person to ask for help or work with on different tasks. They're also better equipped to work under pressure and time constraints; adapting to problems quickly and in a calm manner. As they constantly have to start over, they build resilience and persevere. Games make people feel happier, more productive, more creative, and lower stress levels.

Things to try:

- Laughter therapy
- Watching comedy, standup comedians, writing your own jokes, reading jokes.
- Take an improv comedy class.
- Finding the funny in everything.
- Looking at the situation from an opposite point of view.
- Responding the opposite of what's expected.
- Making others laugh.

---

[44] McGonigal, Jane. *Reality Is Broken: Why Games Make Us Better and How They Can Change the World.* , 2011. Print.

- Smiling often despite how you're feeling.
- Figuring out ways to make whatever you're doing more fun.
- Play more games. Try video games, board games, brain games, all the games you can play.
- Play games at work. Convince your boss to give you time to play games with fellow coworkers and point to the benefits. If you're the boss, then allow your employees to play for some time. It will help your business and their productivity. Try some scenario planning or emergency situation games where employees have to plan out what they would do in different situations in the future, as a team.
- Take all the boring and tedious tasks in your life and gamify them. Have a scoreboard to keep track of how many times you did the dishes, washed the car, mowed the lawn, and took out the trash. Bet some money or have a reward and each week determine who the winner is.
- Use improv comedy ideas your everyday conversations and time with family and friends. It's a great way to have fun, get to know each other better, and get away from the usual way you communicate.
- Think back to when you were a kid. Play the games you did back then. Water balloon fights, super soakers, tag, duck duck goose, hide and seek, etc.

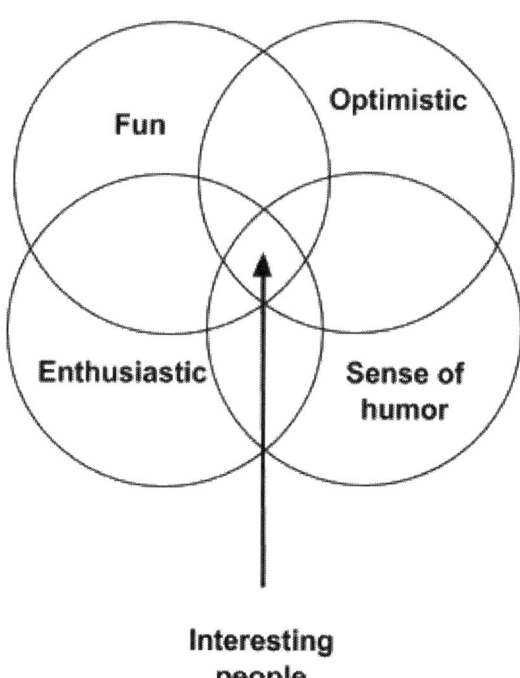

Interesting people

QUESTIONS

- What is funny about this? What isn't and how can you make it funny?
- How can you make this more fun to do? What could you add, subtract, or change in order to make it more fun?
- What if you turned this into a game? What if you turned everything into a game?
- How often do you smile when talking to people? Are you usually more serious?
- What can you do every day to laugh more?

Pushing out of your comfort zone

Tony Robbins says that *"the place where you're most uncomfortable is your comfort zone."*

If you write down all the things that currently make you feel comfortable and those that are making you unhappy, are they related?

What are the things that are making you uncomfortable? Perhaps those are the things you need to actively take action on. Taking necessary action in these areas will move you out of your comfort zone in the shortest period of time. It'll also improve your fulfillment and quality of life.

Once you take a step in that direction, what initially caused fear, is no longer a big issue. Then you can take another step and another. As you do this, you gain momentum. Each step after that becomes easier to take. Beginning is what requires the most effort.

You're in your car waiting for the traffic light to turn green. Once it does, you step on the accelerator and the car starts to move. It takes effort to get the car moving, but once it's moving it gains momentum and can keep moving even if you take your foot off the accelerator. Less gas is used once you're driving at a steady speed. It's the same with you. Once you push past your comfort zone, you'll build momentum, gain more confidence and it'll be easier to keep going.

Most things worth doing are difficult to do. Instant gratification isn't something you'll get when trying to achieve new and challenging objectives. We tend to only hear the good news, the positive side of the story. We don't hear about the pain, the constant struggles, and all the difficulties that people go through.

Many of the things we want in life, can be obtained if we get out of our comfort zone. The further out we step, the more risks we take, the more we learn, the more experience we gain, the more valuable we become to those around us. The more valuable we become, the more quality people we attract. The more great people in our lives, the more we grow. It's a cycle that continues to expand.

It doesn't end there. Think of your comfort zone as concentric circles. You step out of one circle and into a larger one. You get comfortable where you were uncomfortable. You gain a new level. Then you take another step and get comfortable there. Then you go on to the next level. What was once hard, becomes easy. No conclusion, just consistent expansion. Just like the universe is said to be constantly expanding, so should you. If not, you're being inconsistent with nature.

Things to try:

- Choose 5 things that make you uncomfortable in life and cause you pain. Now go and do them. Then make a new

list. If you can't do them on your own, get someone to help and encourage you.
- Use exposure therapy and gradually expose yourself to whatever makes you uncomfortable. Do a little bit every day, until it becomes easy and then make it harder.

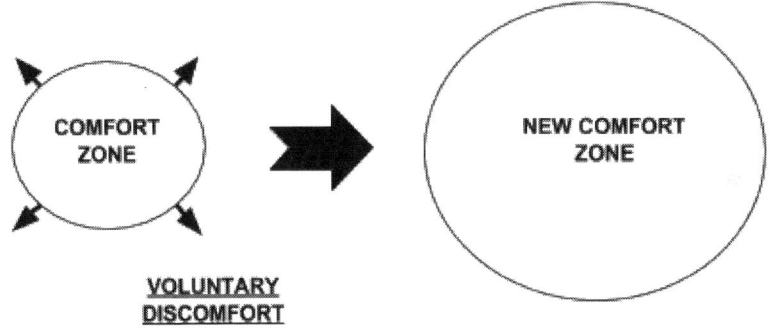

QUESTIONS:

- Where are you most unhappy in your life? What would you need to do to change this around?
- What is it that scares you about doing or achieving certain things? What is it that prevents you from taking that first step?
- What do I fear doing?
- How would my life play out if this weren't an issue?
- How could I do one small thing daily, weekly, or monthly to gradually reduce any feelings of discomfort?
- If pain, stress, and learning from those situations makes me stronger then what can I start doing today, to put myself in those situations?

- What is the worst that can happen if you take action? What is the best that can happen if you take action?

Don't stop pushing yet

> *"I don't count my sit-ups. I only start counting when it starts hurting. When I feel pain, that's when I start counting, because that's when it really counts.*
>
> – Muhammad Ali

When we exercise, we get to a point where we stop even though we might be able to keep going. Perhaps it's how our brain protects us from danger. Just like the light on a car's dashboard lights up when your gas tank is empty. You know there's still enough gas to get to the station.

What we think is our last remaining effort, is not even close. We have more energy than we believe. Next time you begin to think you have nothing more to give, keep going. Push or pull that weight another time, run a little more, read a little more, think a little more. Keep going after you've convinced yourself you're too tired to keep going. Do this regularly and you'll constantly be pushing and challenging yourself to a new a level.

K. Anders Ericsson, in his book, *Peak*,[45] says that top performers are constantly pushing themselves to the edge of their ability. They don't continue to practice what they can already do. Instead, they constantly challenge themselves with more difficult tasks that push them out of their comfort zone and improve their skills.

---

[45] *Peak: Secrets from the New Science of Expertise*. Mariner Books, 2017. Print.

Things to try:

- Get into the habit of never stopping when you feel like it. Say, *"just one more,"* and then go do it. See how far you can push yourself.
- Set a more difficult challenge.

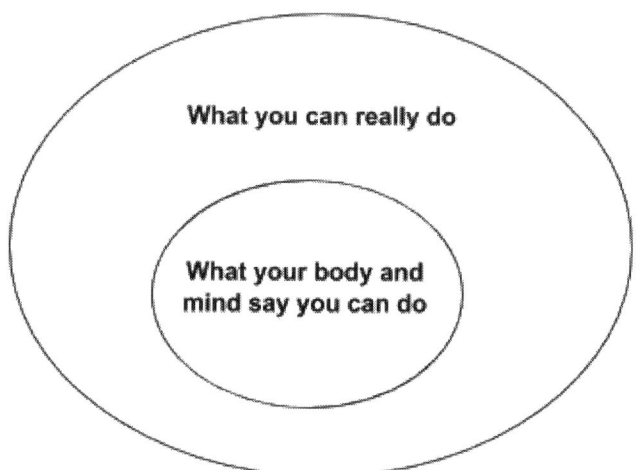

QUESTIONS

- Is this really the best you can do? Can you go farther?
- How much more can you push? How do you know?
- Where do I need to push farther in my life? How can I do that and what would my future be like if I did?
- How can you set a new personal best? What will you need to do in order to keep challenging yourself and moving further?
- How can you turn this into a game and compete with yourself, get better, keep improving?

Getting used to stress

Stressful situations will build your stress tolerance. In, *Antifragile*,[46] Nassim Nicholas Taleb says the opposite of fragile, is antifragile. This means that as a system goes through stress, it will actually get stronger and become more resilient. Your body, for example, when going through a workout; the economy and the periods of recession or a business that goes through hard times and still manages to survive and become stronger.

When you go to the gym, you put strain on your muscles, you break them down, and they ache. This process causes them to harden and strengthen. If you want to keep getting stronger, you have to consistently put them under stress and lift heavier.

Taleb says tranquil environments create fragile systems. In a relationship, when you avoid disagreements and anything that causes a challenge, you may think you're maintaining the harmony. But the moments of tension and challenges lead to growth and create shared experiences that can strengthen your relationship. What we do by trying to keep the peace, is create an emotional flatline which ends up creating a boring relationship.

Challenges and difficulties are a natural part of growth. Any time you choose to move forward there'll be challenges. If you see

---

[46] Taleb, Nassim N. *Antifragile: Things That Gain from Disorder.* , 2016. Print.

these challenges as problems that can't be overcome and panic, you won't be able to enjoy the benefits. By going through the difficulty, we develop the antifragility that creates progress.

We have to embrace volatility instead of trying to reduce it. In *The four-hour work week*, Tim Ferriss says, *"A person's success in life can usually be measured by the number of uncomfortable conversations he or she is willing to have."* [47]

Putting yourself in uncomfortable situations creates stress, but it makes your comfort zone expand. Doing that will allow you to develop courage and the ability to take on bigger challenges.

While stress can have negative effects on your health, what determines the effect it has on your life, is your attitude.

Kelly McGonigal, author of *The upside of stress*,[48] studies stress and helps to bring awareness of the negative effects it has on our health. She did this until coming across a study of how stress could actually be beneficial to our lives. McGonigal investigated further and began to change the way she viewed stress.

These are some of her findings:

- Your stress mindset is what determines whether stress will be helpful or harmful for you. What do you think of

---

[47] Ferriss, Timothy. *The 4-Hour Workweek: Escape 9-5, Live Anywhere, and Join the New Rich*. New York: Harmony Books, 2012. Print.

[48] McGonigal, Kelly. *The Upside of Stress: Why Stress Is Good for You, and How to Get Good at It.* , 2016. Print

stress and how does it affect you, your relationships, and your health?
- You have to understand the downside of stress, but if you focus on the upside, then you will gain more benefits.
- A meaningful life is a stressful life. Often our level of stress is an indicator of how involved we are with everything in our lives.
- Happy lives are not stress free and stress free people do not necessarily live happy lives.

What you believe about stress determines the results it will have on your life. If you see stress as:

- Able to strengthen your willpower
- Challenge you and help you push past your own limits
- Part of the process of learning and growing
- THEN, you'll be able to benefit from it.

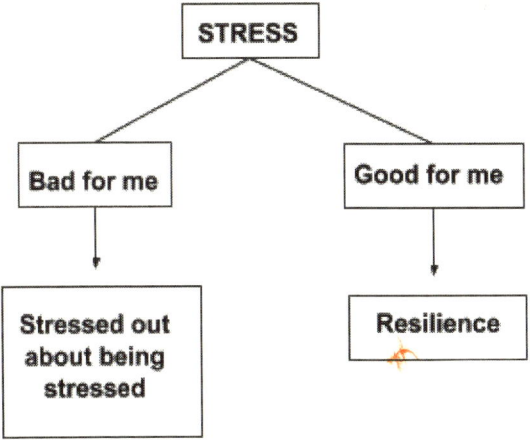

Stress <----> Worry

Stress can lead to worry and worry can lead to stress. What we worry about, often doesn't occur.

Warren Buffett likes to ask, "*Is it knowable and important?*" [49]

- If it's not important and not knowable---> Don't worry about it.
- If it's not important, but knowable---> It's not important, so don't worry about it.
- If it's important, but not knowable ---> Don't worry.
- If it's important and it's knowable ---> Prepare for it beforehand.

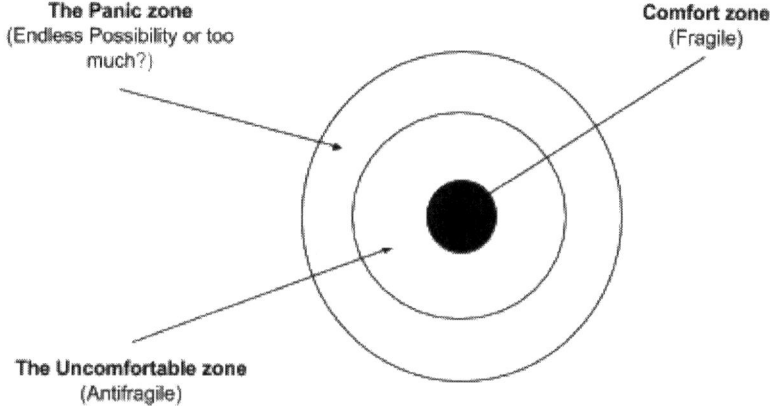

[49] Bevelin, Peter. *Seeking Wisdom: From Darwin to Munger.* Malmö: PCA Publications, 2013. Print.

QUESTIONS

- What are the areas that provide the most meaning\ value in your life? How much stress do they contribute?
- Is the safety and desire to mitigate risk making this system more fragile or antifragile?
- Are you building fragility or antifragility in your life?
- What is causing you the most stress and why? Can it make you more antifragile?
- Are you adding or reducing volatility in your life? What are the consequences or side effects?

Limiting Factors

> *"Limiting factors are an environmental condition like water, food, sunlight, temperature that restrict the types of organisms and population numbers that an environment can support."* [50]

A cactus is not very tall, it loves the sun and can handle extreme heat and cold. The cactus doesn't respond well to high amounts of water, needing only a little to survive. In the desert, the cactus thrives. But if you take the cactus and plant it in a rainforest, everything changes. The tall rainforest trees would block the sun and the cactus would sit in the shade. The soil is different in the rainforest. It's wet and moist. The temperature is also not ideal for a cactus. The cactus's quality and duration of life, depend on where it's located.

The concept of limiting factors is used in biology, but what about our workplace, homes, schools, the places we live, and the relationships we have? What are the limiting factors in your job? Do you work for a company that encourages you to grow, provides constant training and improvement of skills? Is your boss a good leader and will he\ she mentor you to develop your potential? Are you living in a place where there are opportunities in the type of work you want? Are you living in a place with very few opportunities and surrounded by people who aren't encouraging your development? Are you in a relationship with someone who respects you and wants the same things?

---

[50] *Biological Science: A Molecular Approach.* Lexington, Mass: D. C. Heath, 1973. Print.

There are limiting factors in our lives that help us get to where we want or move away from it. We have to know what they are and set things up in a way that'll be beneficial. Placing ourselves in an imaginary rainforest, on purpose, would also push us to develop our ability to adapt and make the best of a difficult situation. The challenge would be an opportunity to test ourselves, grow, and appreciate what we have.

You'll be a result of...

Where you live	What you learn
Who you spend time with	The experiences you go through

QUESTIONS

- Are you a cactus living in a desert? Are you too comfortable? Uncomfortable?
- What benefits can you obtain by placing yourself in a rainforest and suffering a little?
- How can placing yourself in a rainforest give you more appreciation for living in the desert?

Be Willing To Suffer

*"I'm not the strongest. I'm not the fastest.
But I'm really good at suffering."*

-Amelia Boone
(Three-time World's Toughest Mudder Champion)

What are some things that make you uncomfortable and make you suffer? Do one of those things every day. Do them every day for a week or a month, until they're no longer an issue.

If you consistently put yourself in uncomfortable situations where you suffer, you will not only begin to suffer less, but less things will bother you. The tougher and more mentally strong you become, the harder it will be for anything to shake you.

Mark Manson wrote an article titled, *The most important question of your life.*[51] Here is an excerpt:

"If I ask you, "What do you want out of life?" and you say something like, "I want to be happy and have a great family and a job I like," it's so ubiquitous that it doesn't even mean anything...

A more interesting question, a question that perhaps you've never considered before, is what pain do you want in your life? What are

---

[51] Manson, Mark. "The Most Important Question of Your Life." *Mark Manson*, 8 July 2018, markmanson.net/question.

you willing to struggle for? Because that seems to be a greater determinant of how our lives turn out."

What are **you** willing to struggle for?

"PAIN+ REFLECTION = PROGRESS" - Ray Dalio

You only learn the lesson if you reflect on what has happened. Pain alone is not going to do much, unless you look inside and learn from it. Always ask yourself:

What did I learn from this?

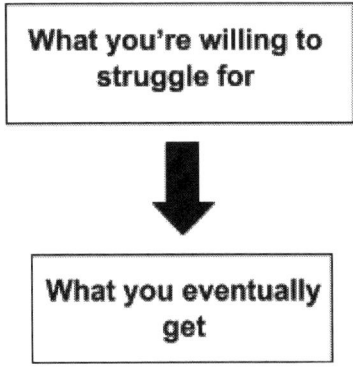

QUESTIONS

- How much are you willing to suffer? How much pain are you willing to endure? How much will you be able to struggle?
- What is making you uncomfortable right now?

- Mark Cuban's question, *"Will you be happy you did this when you're 90?"*
- If you're comfortable doing this, how can you make yourself uncomfortable again?
- How can you increase the challenge and push your ability to the next level?

Emotional control

Staying focused and unemotional in times of stress, is a challenging task. It's hard to make decisions and respond in a positive way, when you're emotional and can't think logically.

One way to learn to control your emotions, is to act out different situations in your mind, before they happen. Come up with a list of possible scenarios and plan out the steps you'd take.

- How would you respond?
- How would things change?
- What would you be able to learn from the situation?
- Who would you talk to?

These kinds of questions will also force you to take a deep look at who your support system is. It will help you focus on finding solutions and let go of focusing on the problems. It will also reduce your emotional reactions should these situations occur in your life.

To keep yourself emotionally under control pause and think things through. Avoid responding immediately if you're angry or if something is bothering you. It's better to stay quiet and take a moment for yourself. Step back, *breathe*, and approach the situation with calm.

Getting proper amounts of sleep, eating well, staying hydrated, and doing physical activity help in maintaining a level of emotional control. If you don't get a good night's rest; if you eat too much sugar or starchy foods, and don't exercise, your response and decision making will suffer.

To control your *anger*, try these ideas from *Angry all the time*, by Ronald T. Potter: [52]

- Don't overreact to problems
- Relax
- Notice other emotions
- Quit trying to control others
- Accept the differences
- Be responsible for your actions and words
- Treat others with respect
- Tell others what bothers you. Be direct, specific and polite

Finding your zone, [53] by Michael Lardon, provides other useful strategies for emotional control:

- When you have time to think before responding, try reframing the issue at hand.
- Accept what you're feeling and transform the energy into something useful.
- Be in the moment. Think of the next move\ play. Avoid dwelling on the past or on what will happen in the future.

---

[52] Potter-Efron, Ronald T. *Angry All the Time: An Emergency Guide to Anger Control.* Oakland, Calif: New Harbinger, 2005. Print.

[53] Lardon, Michael. *Finding Your Zone: Ten Core Lessons for Achieving Peak Performance in Sports and Life.* New York: Perigee Book, 2008. Print.

- Take the thought or emotion that is bothering you and mentally place it on a leaf and let it float down a river.
- Stretch, focus on your breathing, and fix your body posture.
- Think of how you have already gone through this situation before and everything worked out well.
- Substitute your frustration with curiosity. Why is this happening and how could I change it?
- If you're angry, imagine holding a hot piece of coal and then dropping it. As you drop it, feel the anger leaving your body.

Buckets of emotional control

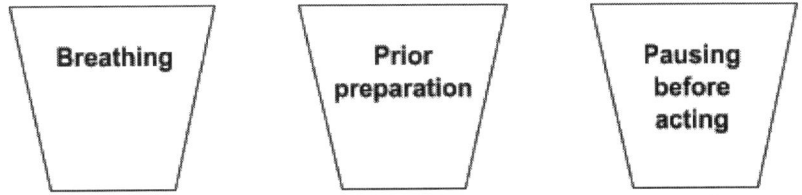

QUESTIONS

- Do you pause and think before speaking? Do you really need to say what you want to say? Does the person need to hear it or do you just want to say it?
- Would responding be useful? Is it necessary?
- Pause and don't say a word. Keep it to yourself.
- Are you focusing on your breathing?

- Have you prepared for different scenarios? What will you do if something you didn't prepare for occurs?
- Is this something you can control or is it outside your control?
- What can you learn from this?
- Can you let others have their own opinion and stay quiet, even if they're uninformed?

Rejection

"It turns out, it's not the number of hits or home runs we get that matters; we can instead manifest our success by simply stepping up to the plate more often."

-Neil Patel

It will happen in every aspect of our lives; at work, in relationships, school, sports, whatever you do.

Anything we want to achieve is going to have obstacles along the way. These obstacles are a necessary part of the process. In going through these obstacles you develop the skills needed to get to the next level. That is the way. Among these obstacles you'll have to go through rejection. Humans fear rejection. We relate rejection with being thrown out of the tribe. To our ancestors, this would mean the loss of our social circle, the protection of the group, less access to food, and most likely death.

We no longer live under the same circumstances.

If you don't take rejection personally, you can grow and learn from it. When you get rejected by someone, ask them why. That way you can improve your approach and better position yourself for success.

You never really know why others will reject you. Maybe there's no interest in your proposition. Maybe they're going through a difficult moment in their lives and it's just bad timing. Unless you ask and they tell you, you won't really know.

Rejection is a test you have to go through. In order to get what you want, you have to go through it. If you don't do it, your life won't change. If you aren't happy with the way things are, you'll need to face rejection and learn to love the process. See it for what it is. A necessary phase of life. Another learning stage.

Are you willing to get rejected countless times to get what you want?

Michael Jordan didn't get chosen for his high school basketball team. This gave him the motivation to improve his basketball skills. He went on to become one of the greatest basketball players of all time.

Sometimes you get rejected simply because you are ahead of your time. Charles Darwin and Copernicus had theories that went against the old way of seeing the world. The theory of evolution and a world where the earth revolved around the sun and not the other way around were completely against the thinking of the time. The church protested and opposed their ideas. Today, these ideas have scientific evidence to support them and are no longer considered far out.

Things to try:

- Ask people: What did I do right? What do I need to improve and how? Ask others the same questions and work to improve. The more rejections you get, the less

fear you'll feel and the more you can improve. Treat rejection like a game.
- The player that gets up to bat 1000 times, can hit more singles than the one who goes to bat only 10 times.
- Try cold calling, door to door sales, going up to people you're attracted to, talking to them and getting their contact info.
- Ask people to participate in random activities with you or ask them for random favors.

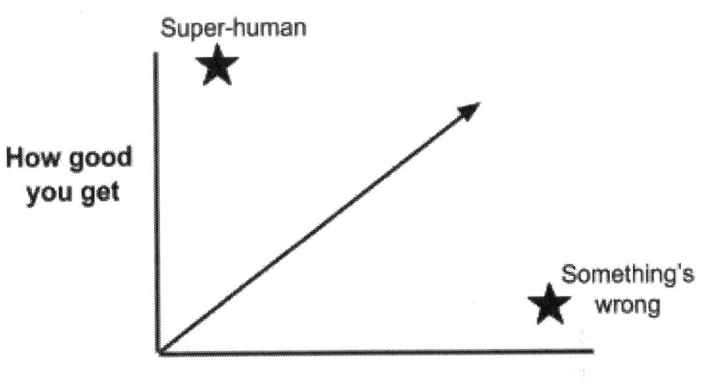

QUESTIONS

- What can you learn from the rejection? Why were you rejected?
- What can you do better next time that would reduce probability of rejection?

- How many times have you tried and how many have you been rejected?
- After a certain amount of rejection, feedback and trying again, what results do you get? At this point does rejection bother you less or more?
- What can you do to make sure you get rejected?
- Is there something wrong with you or can it be that the other person isn't having a good day?
- What are some things you can do, to get over rejection?
- Pretend the worst has already happened. How do you feel? How do you act?

Embracing failure

> *"I've missed more than 9,000 shots in my career. I've lost almost 300 games. 26 times, I've been trusted to take the game-winning shot and missed. I've failed over and over and over again in my life. And that is why I succeed."*
>
> -Michael Jordan

Failure has a received a bad reputation. Try looking at it from another perspective by giving it another name. Some synonyms could be:

- Learning, Experience, Challenge, Revenue

Jack Ma, founder of Alibaba says, *"failure is revenue."*

Failure is experience and the more failure you have, provided you learn from it, the better you'll be. Every step you take towards your goals, reveals something that will get you closer to them. Look at it this way and the moments of struggle, will be your best teachers. Learn the lesson and move forward.

> Trial and error ---> New learning ---> Improvement

We need to let go of the 'not yet' approach. We wait for things to be perfect and delay taking action because it's 'not yet' time. This keeps going and we end up not taking action to avoid failing.

John Maxwell in, *Failing Forward*,[54] states that the average entrepreneur takes 3.8 tries before they have a successful business. Most of us never hear of the failures, but only the successes. Furthermore, for every person's success story, there are far more stories of failure.

Quantity trumps quality, when it comes to producing great work.

In, *Art and fear*,[55] David Boyles and Ted Orland mention a study performed in a Ceramics class at a university. The teacher divided the students into two groups. One group had to make one ceramic pot and would be graded on its quality. The other group would be graded based on the quantity of pots they created. The teacher would weigh their work on a scale. What group do you think ended up making the best pot?

The first group worked a long time on one pot. The second group, produced a large number of pots, improved their skills, and learned from mistakes as they created each new pot. As a result, the group who created more quantity, created higher quality work and received the higher grade.

---

[54] Maxwell, John C. *Failing Forward: How to Make the Most of Your Mistakes.* Thomas Nelson Publishers, 2000. Print.

[55] Bayles, David, and Ted Orland. *Art & Fear: Observations on the Perils (and Rewards) of Artmaking.* Santa Cruz, CA: Image Continuum Press, 2016. Print.

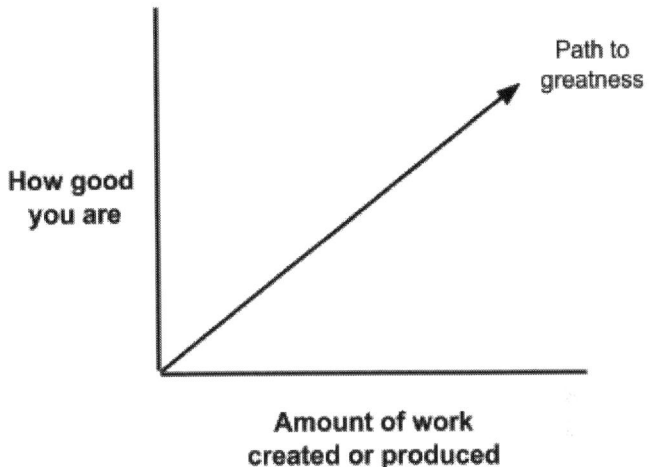

Our fear of failing also comes from our fear of looking foolish doing something new. But that is exactly what we need to do, in order to reach success. We need to be okay with being a beginner. Emptying our cup and starting from scratch.

All the mistakes and screw ups, eventually, lead to success. For that to happen, you have to try many times. The more you try, the more you'll learn.

If you do it, no matter the quality, you'll be able to learn something and move forward. If you don't do it, you'll stay in the same place. It's better to do it and do it fast. The faster you fail, the faster you learn.

If at first you don't succeed, try again; have a backup plan.

Prepare the scenarios ahead of time and have many paths to get to where you want. The more scenarios you think through, the better equipped you'll be to outmaneuver obstacles. Use the pre-mortem, think ahead, and put your current ideas and beliefs out of business consistently to anticipate change. You'll gain peace of mind in knowing that whatever happens, you won't be surprised and can get back on course.

Be like a product designer. Come up with an idea, create a prototype, put it to the test, get feedback, make the necessary improvements, and repeat.

Things to try:

- Try something and then try it again. Then do it again, until it works out. Go up to bat as many times as necessary to hit a single.
- Then try something harder. Keep challenging yourself.
- Learn every step of the way by reflecting.

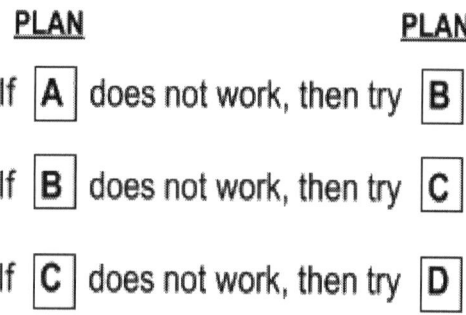

QUESTIONS

- Have I failed enough times to develop some competence in this field?
- Have I failed more times than the average person has tried?
- Am I seeing failure as a path to success?
- What am I failing at in my life right now that will eventually lead me to success?
- What did I fail at today?
- What would you do in spite of the probability of failure?

The Stoic Philosophy

The stoics were philosophers who believed you should focus on what you could control and accept that which you could not. They sought to achieve a life of virtue and tranquility and believed that the path to happiness and wisdom, was through the study of philosophy.

Stoics focus on internal rather than external goals. For example, when playing tennis, you can't control whether you win the game. That is an external goal. Instead, you can choose to focus on what you do control: *playing to the best of your ability*. Detaching from the external goal, allows you to play a great match and sometimes, still win.

Some useful techniques you can borrow from the Stoics:

1- Make a list of what you control and what you don't.

William B. Irvine in, *A guide to the good life*,[56] suggests making a list of all the things you control and those you don't. Create internal goals for all those which you don't control.

Eric Potterat, a clinical psychologist used to work with Navy SEALS and now trains people to perform under pressure.[57] He draws a big circle on a board and asks people the following:

---

[56] Irvine, William B. *A Guide to the Good Life: The Ancient Art of Stoic Joy*. Oxford [etc.]: Oxford University Press, 2009. Print.

[57] Bercovici, Jeff. *Play on : the new science of elite performance at any age*. Boston: Houghton Mifflin Harcourt, 2018. Print.

- List the causes that make you stressed when you're performing. What happens in those situations?
- Which of those is external and outside your control?
- Inside the circle he writes, *"things I control: my attitude, my effort, my actions."* Those are internal.
- Potterat reminds people that when things get difficult you should, *"Stay in your circle."*

2- Negative visualization

Consider what you value in your life and what it'd be like, if you were to lose it. What would you feel, if you lost someone you loved? If you lost your dominant arm and were no longer able to play a sport? If you could no longer walk? How would you feel if a relationship ended, or if the health you enjoy today, gave way to disease?

3- Voluntary discomfort

Choosing to be uncomfortable on purpose. Dressing in rags and spending the evening on the street. Not eating for a day or two to know what hunger feels like. Taking an ice cold shower. Wearing more clothing during the summer or less clothing during the winter to experience the weather at a more intense level.

Voluntary discomfort is about taking the harder path, making the harder choice, and using that to toughen up.

In an interview with Tim Ferriss, General Stanley McChrystal refers to something similar called, shared privation. This is used as a way to develop mental toughness.

McChrystal says, *"put yourself in groups who share difficulties, discomfort. We used to call it 'shared privation.' [Definition of privation: a state in which things essential for human well-being such as food and warmth are scarce or lacking.] You'll find that when you have been through that kind of difficult environment, you feel more strongly about that which you're committed to."* [58]

4- Memento Mori

Latin for "remember death" or "remember that you have to die." This is a constant reminder of our mortality. The Stoics used death as a way to give perspective to life. Our time on earth is limited. Know what's important to you and live your life in accordance with that because you never know when it'll end.

5- "Be stingy with your time." - Seneca

Time, once it's gone doesn't come back. Use it for things that matter and the people who are important. In studies done with elderly people,[59] they all agree that what they regret most, is not what they did in their life, but what they didn't do.

If you only had six months to live, what would you do with your life? What would you change? If it's not in line with the life you live now, maybe you need to change how you spend your time.

---

[58] Ferriss, Tim. "General Stan McChrystal on Eating One Meal Per Day, Special Ops, and Mental Toughness." *The Blog of Author Tim Ferriss*, 28 Sept. 2017, tim.blog/2015/07/05/stanley-mcchrystal/.

[59] Ware, Bronnie. *The Top Five Regrets of the Dying: A Life Transformed by the Dearly Departing.*, 2013. Print

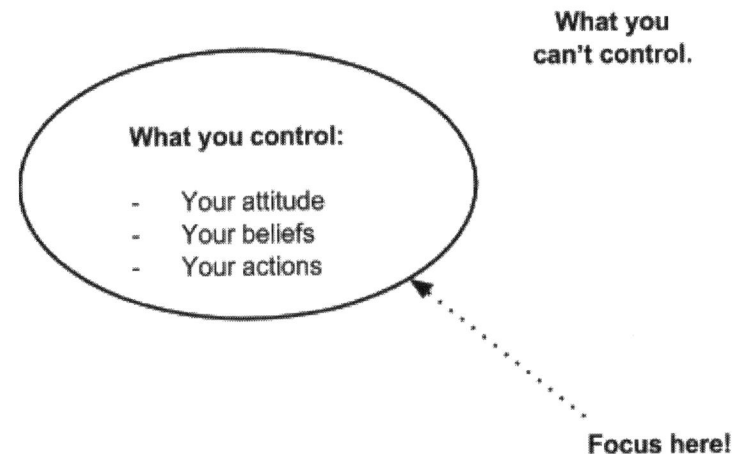

QUESTIONS

- Where can you apply negative visualization?
- What parts of life do you need to be more stoic?
- Where and how can you practice voluntary discomfort?
- How will choosing the harder choice benefit you?
- What can you learn\ apply from the Stoics to your life today? This year?
- How can Stoicism change the way you look at your past?
- What in your life are you not appreciating enough?
- Are you focused on what you control?
- How are you spending your time? Is it leading you to where you want?

Insecurity & Uncertainty

"The task we must set for ourselves is not to feel secure, but to be able to tolerate insecurity."

-Erich Fromm

We want to control everything in our lives. To create certainty so only what we want, occurs. But it doesn't work that way. We have to embrace the uncertainty and insecurity in our life.

Alan Watts in, *The wisdom of insecurity*,[60] says you'll find immense pleasure in falling in love with someone. There's always the risk, however, that you'll fall out of love. One of you will want something, or someone different. Maybe you'll want to take different paths. What first brought you pleasure, now brings you pain. Both feelings are temporary and necessary parts of life.

In, *Foolproof*,[61] Greg Ip discusses how our desire to make things safer, can make them dangerous. For example, safety regulations in sports have caused an adverse effect. Helmets in American football and Ice Hockey reduced the amount of head injuries, but increased the amount of spine injuries. The Federal Reserve seeks to control inflation and protect the US economy, yet the measures it took prior to the 2008 economic crisis, made things worse. Anti-Lock brakes caused drivers to actually take more risks with

---

[60] Watts, Alan. *The Wisdom of Insecurity: A Message for an Age of Anxiety.*, 2011. Print

[61] Ip, Greg. *Foolproof: Why Safety Can Be Dangerous and How Danger Makes Us Safe.*, 2015. Print.

their cars. They started driving faster, taking curves at higher speeds, and accidents increased.

Our search for stability often ends up creating instability. We want to avoid disaster, but end up causing more minor and frequent damage.

Sometimes the more in danger we feel, the safer we are. In flying, there is a zero risk tolerance policy. People's fear of flying has forced airlines to take precautions to ensure maximum safety. Flying, despite the fear some people feel, is the safest way to travel.

You have to accept that maybe you're wrong, maybe you're right. No one truly knows what the future holds. We can predict, but we can't be 100% certain. If we're certain, we close ourselves off to all the possibilities out there.

In, *The power of Uncertainty*,[62] Susan Jeffers says that our desire to feel certain, comes from our need to be right about things. Once we let go of the need to be right, we realize how much we don't know, and how much we can't control.

Try the 'Maybe exercise' from Susan Jeffers book:

- Take any statement you say with certainty and add "*maybe*" at the end.

---

[62] Jeffers, Susan J. *Embracing uncertainty : breakthrough methods for achieving peace of mind when facing the unknown.* New York: St. Martin's Griffin, 2004. Print.

For example: *This trip is going to be amazing...maybe.*

- You can also substitute "*maybe*" for "*it will*" or "*it won't.*"

For example: *This trip is going to be amazing. Maybe it will or maybe it won't.*

Another suggestion Jeffers shares is to learn from any positive or negative situation.

- Ex: My trip wasn't fun.
  What can I learn from this?

- Ex: When I travel, spending time with the locals is what I enjoy the most.
  What can I learn from this?

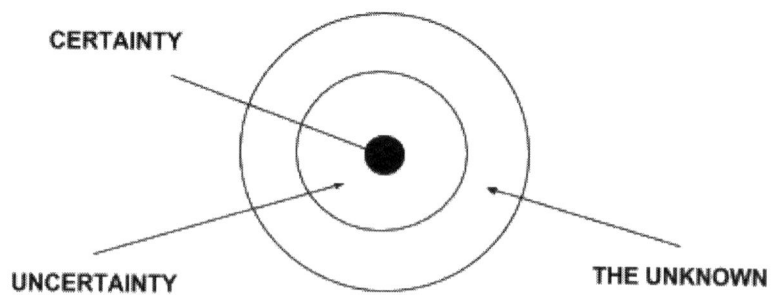

QUESTIONS

- Where in your life can you apply the power of maybe?

- Are you creating a false sense of safety or certainty by making this safer?
- What is the risk and reward?
- If I make this safer, will I take unnecessary risks in another area?
- What about this situation or solution, is uncertain? What is the certainty in this situation?
- How can I embrace the uncertainty and prepare for it?
- What can I learn here?
- Am I focusing on being right or on learning something new? Is it possible I am missing something?
- What have I not considered?

Attachment & Detachment

Being detached means you aren't tied to any particular outcome. When you have something you expect to happen or a belief of how things should be, you become vulnerable when things don't go according to plan. Attachment means you're tied to something. It could be a person, place, thing or an idea. It could be a specific outcome.

If you can't accept other ways of seeing the world; other opinions that are valuable, then you're attached to your own beliefs. If you have a hard time letting go of possessions, you're also attached.

The 5 levels of attachment,[63] by Don Miguel Ruiz Jr. discusses how far we can go in our attachment:

- Level one- The Authentic self: You enjoy the moment without any attachment.
- Level two- Preference: You attach, but can detach easily.
- Level three- Identity: You are attached to it. You identify with it. It partly defines who you are.
- Level four- Internalization: It's a part of who you are. You impose it on others and relate only to those who believe the same thing.
- Level five- Fanaticism: It's who you are and defines you completely.

---

[63] Ruiz, Jr. Don Miguel. *Five Levels of Attachment*. Place of publication not identified: Hierophant Publishing, 2015. Print

Ruiz says that we have different levels in different areas of our lives. Our levels of attachment can be uncovered by questioning our own assumptions. If you think anyone who doesn't believe in your religion is not worth spending time with, then you're very attached to your religious beliefs. If you have friends who follow different religions and are able to relate with them, without it being a problem, then you're not too attached to your beliefs. The lower levels of attachment keep you open to different ideas, possibilities, and help you better understand the world.

Here are some steps to learn to detach from *Let go now, Embracing Detachment:* [64]

- Give up on specific outcomes and be open to what happens.
- Be a spectator of what is happening. Avoid responding unless you really want to.
- Let go. Avoid trying to control anything.
- Do nothing.
- Avoid letting other people's behavior cause you to suffer. If you do suffer, that is your choice.
- Don't let other people control you.
- Let go of the need for approval.
- Let others have their own opinion and be open to it. You may learn something.
- Don't depend on other people in order to be happy.
- Evaluate whether thinking about something is good for you or not.
- Be willing to just walk away.

---

[64] Casey, Karen. *Let Go Now: Embracing Detachment.* San Francisco: Conari Press, 2010. Internet resource.

- Step back and look at life from a distance.
- Live your life, not someone else's.
- Change what you can and accept that which you can't.
- Challenge your assumptions. Find the holes in your beliefs. Fill them with more understanding and acceptance.

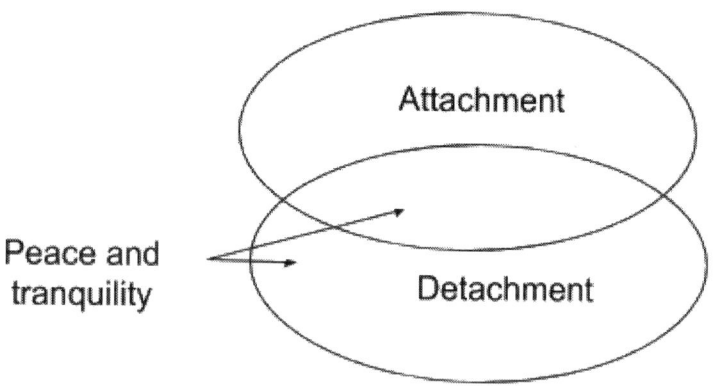

QUESTIONS

- What did you discover or realize about yourself?
- What does this mean?
- How could I use this to get better?
- Who would benefit from learning this?
- Is this useful to you? Useful for someone else?
- What can you learn here?
- Is there something you're missing or not seeing? Hidden unknowns?
- Is there a better way? Is this a better way?

- Are you attached to specific outcomes?
- Are you able to just walk away from this?
- How can you detach from different situations and things in your life?
- Are you placing your happiness in someone else's hands?
- Is it a good idea for you to think about this? Can you just walk away and let it go?
- What do you need to accept and come to terms with?

Patience

Don't expect results immediately or rush things to fruition before their time. Anything worthwhile takes hard work and patience. It also takes time. View everything as a work in progress; slowly, but constantly evolving.

The fastest path, is not necessarily, the shortest distance. In, *Hustle*,[65] Neil Patel discusses the advantages and disadvantages of travelling by boat, on the Gulf Stream. An ocean current that originates in the Gulf of Mexico and travels up the North American coast until crossing the Atlantic Ocean, into Europe and Africa. Boats travelling from the United States to England will arrive much faster if they use it. Boats travelling in the opposite direction will find their journey much longer. While the Gulf Stream is not the shortest path in terms of distance to get from North America to Europe, it is the fastest route in terms of time and speed.

Perhaps being patient and taking the seemingly slower route, is the fastest path to get where you want.

Things to improve your patience:

- Focus on your breathing and enjoying the present moment

---

[65] Patel, Neil, Patrick Vlaskovits, and Jonas Koffler. *Hustle: The Power to Charge Your Life with Money, Meaning, and Momentum.* , 2016. Internet resource.

- If you feel impatient, ask yourself if that feeling is helping you move toward what you want or not.
- Use the If-then statements. "If I get impatient or want instant gratification, then I'll take a deep breath and focus on what I can control."
- Take it easy. Go slow. Don't rush.
- Ask yourself, "what would a patient person do?"
- Pause and think things through before responding.
- Work on delaying gratification. Don't immediately give in to what you desire. Make yourself wait.
- Focus on the process and hitting your hourly and daily tasks.
- Read stories of people who are successful. Study their lives and find out how long it took them to get to where they wanted. This will encourage you and add perspective.

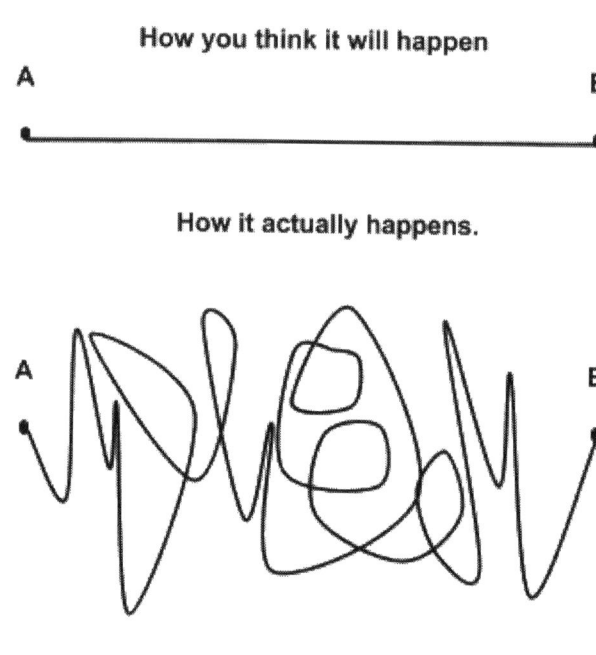

QUESTIONS

- How can you improve your self-control so you can be more patient, think things through and not make impulsive decisions?
- Why can you not delay gratification? What keeps you from it?
- What is an example of not being patient in your life? What would be different if you were patient?
- If you improve your patience where would you be in a few weeks? Months?

Hard choices

"There are always two choices. Two paths to take. One is easy. And it's only reward is that it's easy."
—Unknown

If you have to make a choice between two paths and one is more difficult, choose the harder one. Challenge yourself. Make things harder on purpose. Hard choices have a way of making us more resilient. All the hard choices we make and go through, prepare us better for the future.

When you find yourself going for the easy choice, ask yourself why. Think longer term. What are the consequences of picking the easier option? What would happen as a result of picking the harder choice? Where are there more pros than cons?

Taking the harder path will strengthen you and make it difficult for obstacles to bring you to a standstill. It will strengthen your character and frustration will become second-nature. The harder choice may be slower, but it will bring more rewards.

"Hard Choices, Easy Life. Easy Choices, Hard Life."
—Jerzy Gregory

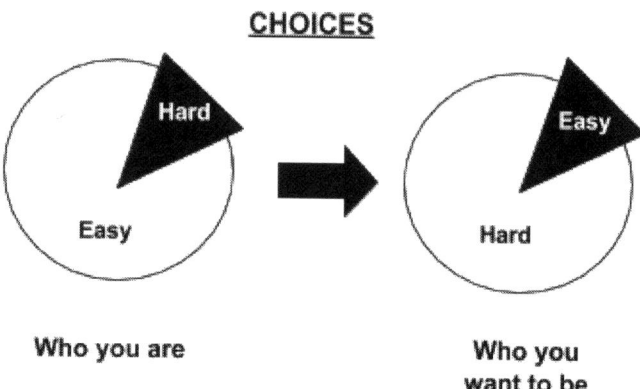

The relationships you build

The people in your life will learn from you and you'll learn from them. Pick them well.

Aside from family, a variety of people from different age groups, different cultures, different types of jobs, interests and beliefs, is a great way to expose yourself to what you don't know. Build diversity into your group. Take advantage of the wisdom of the crowd and learn from everyone.

Steven Johnson, in his TED talk, *Where good ideas come from*, discusses how coffee houses played an important role in the enlightenment. Johnson says, *"they were places where people would come together from different backgrounds and different fields of expertise and share. It was a space...where ideas could have sex."*[66]

If the people around you challenge you to think about things in different ways and constantly challenge you to be better, then you'll be forced to grow. If we only relate with people similar to us, we limit the amount of new ideas.

Everyone has a definition of what a good friend means. Look for those who encourage you and help you move forward. People who are honest with you, hold you accountable, and provide new and different opinions. A good friend is a coach who tells you when you're doing things well and lets you know when you mess up. A

---

[66] Johnson, Steven. "Where Good Ideas Come from | Steven Johnson." *YouTube*, TED, 21 Sept. 2010, www.youtube.com/watch?v=0af00UcTO-c.

good friend is also a cheerleader who encourages you no matter how terrible you're playing. They balance a mix of truth, encouragement, and guidance.

Jim Rohn used to say, *"you're the average of the 5 people you spend the most time with."* Who are the five people closest to you? The ones you spend most of your time with?

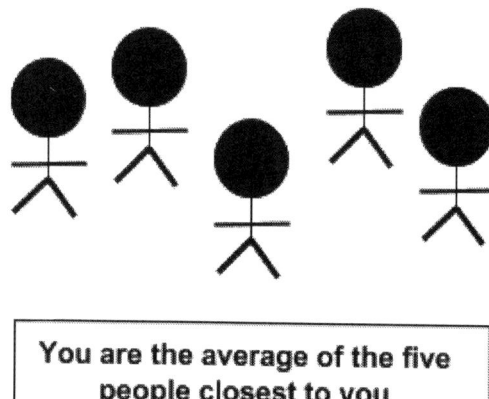

You are the average of the five people closest to you

When you first begin dating someone, you meet their closest friends. It can feel like an audition. Will they approve or disapprove of me? While this may be uncomfortable, it has a benefit. You get to meet the people they spend most of their time with. By getting to know their friends, you also get to know the person you're dating. After some time, you're able to decide if they're good company. The more time you spend with them, the more similar you become. That can determine whether or not you'll pursue the relationship.

James Altucher recommends having a plus, minus, equal.[67] The plus is someone who's at a higher level and can teach you or mentor you. They serve as a guide who challenges, gives you feedback and helps you improve. The equal is someone who is at your same level. A boxer may have a sparring partner who is at their same level of ability. They practice the new skills they're learning, work out together, and push each other to improve. The minus is someone you can teach and help to develop. A younger boxer, for example, that you can mentor.

To better connect with people, try these ideas:

- Begin with yourself. Learn to see the potential in people. See them for who they could become and treat them that way. When you treat people as if they are the person they could be or want to be, you help encourage them to become that person.
- Ask yourself how you can help other people.
- Think of the most important people in your life and write down 3 things you can do each week to strengthen your relationship.
- Offer help and give. Consider how you can add the most value to their lives. By doing this, you'll be able to ask for their help when you're in need of it.
- Relationships, like a strong and healthy body, take time and patience to develop. They can't be forced.

---

[67] Altucher, James. *Reinvent Yourself.* , 2016. Print.

- If you want to get to know people do a fun activity with them. In those moments people are more relaxed and sincere.
- Go deeper than small talk. In order for this to happen you need to actually have something to say. You need thoughts of your own. Educate yourself, read, and learn.
- Learn to listen. Remember that sometimes, *"it's better to be interested, than interesting."* People love to talk about themselves.
- To nurture relationships contact people daily and be sociable. Send a message, a joke, video, letter, email, voice message, a compliment, some words of affirmation, a gift, spend time with them, call them, or go out with them.
- Set up mastermind dinners and networking events.
- Reach out to influencers or people you look up to through email or social media.
- When you add the right people to your circle, you benefit from their strengths and are able to learn from them.
- Connect with super connectors; people who have huge networks. It takes the same amount of effort as connecting with someone who has a small network.

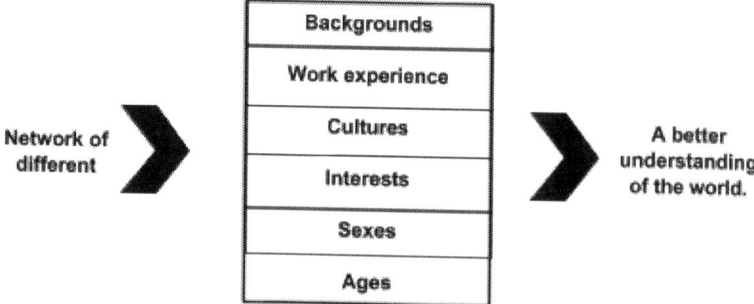

QUESTIONS

- How much diversity and variety is there in your social group? Different work, ages, sexes, backgrounds, perspectives?
- Do they question and disagree or do they just agree?
- Are they people that add value or subtract? Do they help you move closer to who you want to be?
- Who are your plus, minus and equal?
- Is there someone there that you can mentor? Someone who can mentor you? Someone with an equal ability level who can challenge you?
- Who do you challenge and engage in conversations with? Who could you engage in conversations with and why don't you? Can you do something today to begin creating a relationship?
- Who are you becoming by spending time with this person? With all these people?
- Do they challenge you? Lift you up? Bring you down?
- Where can you go to meet the type of people you want to meet?
- Who do you have around you that is supporting what you're trying to accomplish? Are they people that ask you how they can help you when you tell them what you want out of life?

PART 5 - Implementing the ideas

Deliberate Practice

K. Anders Ericsson, Krampe, and Tesch-Romer performed a now well known study with violin students from the West Berlin Music Academy.[68] The music professors divided the groups of violinists into 3 groups. The first group, called "the best students" were the most likely to have careers as international soloists or play in top symphony orchestras. The second group was referred to as "the good students." The third group were violinists who studied music education and were called "the music teachers." The students were all about the same ages and had on average, started studying violin at 8 years old.

Some of the conclusions were:

- Great performance isn't something that happens due to great talent, but a result of focused, deliberate practice time.

- At age 18, the best students had accumulated an average of 7,410 hours of deliberate practice. The good students had accumulated 5,301 hours on average and the music teachers 3,420 hours.

---

[68] Ericsson, K. Anders. "The Role of Deliberate Practice in the Acquisition of Expert Performance." American Psychological Association, 1993, graphics8.nytimes.com/images/blogs/freakonomics/pdf/DeliberatePractice(PsychologicalReview).pdf.

To become a top performer in any area requires focused practice time and consistent feedback from an experienced mentor\teacher.

In Ericsson's book, *Peak*, he points out some key points of deliberate practice:

- Purposeful training means learning not just by knowing, but also by doing. You have to understand the theory, but active teaching and learning strategies are better for learning than classroom learning.

- You need an expert instructor or mentor to guide you and learn from.

- The student must be pushed past their ability level. Skills will plateau if not pushed to a higher level.

- The length of practice does not guarantee high level expertise. It is the quality of focused, deliberate practice over time that will produce expertise.

- It is never too late to learn new things.

- With the right training and practice, a person with not much talent, can improve and become better than a talented person.

- Mental training is just as important as physical training.

How to practice

Learning to practice can be a long and frustrating process. I suggest you set apart 15-30 minutes a day to apply some of the ideas provided in the book, answer the questions, and do the activities in the "things to try" section. Spending 15-30 minutes daily in a focused manner will do more for you in the long run than:

    A- Never doing anything at all
    B- Kind of doing some of the exercises
    C- Trying to do too much all at once
    D- Hours of unfocused practice

Make sure to keep track of your progress, seek feedback from others, and stay objective. Pay attention to your strengths and areas that need improvement. The better you understand yourself and your personal needs, the more clearly you'll understand what you need to work on. Focus on what you consider most important for you.

Practice the concepts in this book in different situations. Use them while thinking about your life or in conversation with other people. Use them to think in a different way and find alternate points of view. Apply them to different areas of your life.

Lastly, have as much fun as you can with the ideas. If they aren't fun, you won't enjoy using them. Think of different ways to make a game out of them. Use them every chance you get and they'll become a part of who you are and how you think.

Sample Ideas

The following ideas are a jumping off point. Spend a specific amount of focused time working on them. Spend each day practicing a different idea or work on the same one for a week. It's up to you. Try using deliberate practice and then just have fun. The important thing is to put them to use consistently, to continuously push past your current ability level, and to measure your progress.

- Choose one topic and work on the questions and 'things to try' section. Do one topic per day. Use it as much as you can, wherever you can apply it.

- Take the ideas in the putting things in perspective section and think of how they apply to different situations or events you come across.

- Ask a minimum number of questions every day. Ask yourself, your friends, family, coworkers, or strangers. Get curious about what you don't know about them.

- Read some questions on www.quora.com and think of how you could apply one of the concepts in this book to people's challenges. Spend 15-30 minutes coming up with ideas of how that concept could help. Answer some people's questions.

- Spend 15-30 minutes applying it to your life in specific challenges or problem areas. Your work, health, relationships, etc. Consider different situations your friends or family members are going through as well.

- Go through an international news site and read all the headlines. Consider how the concepts could apply to different situations.

- Place each idea on a notecard. Take them with you everywhere you go. Review them daily considering what you can apply in different situations that you come across.

- Take one specific challenge in your life and apply each concept to it to determine what you had not seen and where you have an opportunity.

- Place yourself in situations that require you to use a certain skill.

- Whatever you're working on, list things that could go wrong and how you would respond.

- Create challenges for yourself in different areas of your life (health, work, relationships, etc) and figure out how you can achieve them. Then go for it. Once you achieve them, set more difficult challenges and develop the skills to achieve those.

-
- Use Plutchik's wheel daily to determine how you're feeling. Try it in the morning, afternoon and evening. Keep track of what you're feeling and why. Use the ideas in the book to move from negative to positive emotions.

- Meditate daily. Focus on your breathing.

- Study the life of one person you admire for a day, week or month and consider what they would do, think and how they would act in different circumstances.

- Take a list of problems in the world and your life and come up with all the solutions you can think of.

- Join a competition in something that interests you. Practice with someone who is better than you.

- Go for a walk every day. Walk faster than usual and disconnect.

- Take different decisions you have to make and consider the long term consequences. Consider the long term consequences of current events in the news.

- Sign up for a class in something you've never done.
- Do something to get you rejected every day.

- Make a list of tests and experiments to try in different areas of your life and do one daily. Write down what you expect to happen and compare it to what happens.

- Come up with as many different perspectives as you can for every situation you encounter.

Conclusion

To create continued interest in your life, Mikhail Csikszentmihalyi, says you have to make it more complex. Make it more challenging and then force yourself to develop new abilities to match that level of challenge. By constantly exploring and expanding we'll maintain interest in any area we desire. When we become complacent and stop being curious, we get bored and lose interest. Learn to look at everything in your life, with completely new eyes. It's my hope that this book gives you the ability to do that.

At the beginning of the book, you listed what was important to you, what you wanted out of life, the person you wanted to become, and the reasons for doing what you do. You now have a bag filled with tools that'll get you from point A to point B, despite the obstacles you'll find along your path. If you put in the work, they'll get you where you want and show you how to enjoy the ride.

NOW, is a good time to start.

SHARE & REVIEW

Thanks for taking the time to read the book and getting to the end. You have plenty of books to choose from and I'm grateful you gave this book a chance. If you've found the ideas useful, gained new perspectives and tools that helped you, then I'd like to ask you for a favor. Could you help spread the word by writing a review on Amazon and share your thoughts with friends and family?

This lets me continue to create quality work that helps many people.

"Knowledge, when shared, is like a high tide; it raises all boats."

Thanks so much!

List of people to study

Business

- Oprah Winfrey
- Sheryl Sandberg
- Arianna Huffington
- Sara Blakely
- Elizabeth Arden
- Barbara Corcoran
- Lori Greiner
- Rockefeller
- Andrew Carnegie
- T. Boone Pickens
- Richard Branson
- Henry Ford
- Mark Cuban
- Bill Gates
- Steve Jobs
- Warren Buffett
- Charlie Munger
- Elon Musk
- Jeff Bezos
- Sam Walton
- Ray Kroc
- Colonel Sanders
- Jack Ma
- Sakichi Toyoda
- Larry Page
- Phil Knight
- Mark Zuckerberg
- Donald Trump
- Estee Lauder
- John Paul DeJoria
- Ray Dalio
- Daymond John
- Chris Sacca
- Peter Drucker
- Ken Robinson
- Jim Collins
- Clayton Christensen
- Tom Peters
- John Paul Getty
- Michael Bloomberg
- Li Ka Shing
- Scott Belsky

Philosophers

- Plato
- Aristotle
- Socrates
- Immanuel Kant
- Rene Descartes
- Friedrich Nietzsche
- Jean Jacques Rousseau
- Thomas Aquinas
- Confucius
- Voltaire
- Kierkegaard
- Arthur Schopenhauer

- Epicurus
- Albert Camus
- Alan Watts
- Thoreau
- Seneca
- Lao Zi
- Sigmund Freud
- Buddha
- Marcus Aurelius
- Plutarch
- Marcel Proust
- Heraclitus
- Alain de Botton

Spiritual Leaders

- Pope Francis
- The 14th Dalai Lama
- Desmond Tutu
- Don Miguel Ruiz
- Thich Nhat Hanh
- Osho
- Jiddu Krishnamurti
- Mother Teresa
- Mahatma Gandhi
- Sai Baba of Shirdi
- Swami Vivekananda

Presidents, leaders, generals, revolutionaries

- Alexander the Great
- George Washington
- Che Guevara
- Eisenhower
- Genghis Khan
- Joan of Arc
- William Wallace
- Adolf Hitler
- Douglas MacArthur
- Francisco Franco
- Charles de Gaulle
- Napoleon Bonaparte
- Colin Powell
- William Sherman
- Sun Zi (Sun Tzu)
- Sitting Bull
- Isoroku Yamamoto
- Simon Bolivar
- Carl von Clausewitz
- Abraham Lincoln
- Niccolo Machiavelli
- Karl Marx
- Nelson Mandela
- Winston Churchill
- Lyndon B. Johnson
- Augusto Pinochet
- Jose Mujica
- Julius Caesar
- Cyrus the Great

Sports Coaches

- Dan Gable
- John Wooden
- Bill Belichick
- Phil Jackson
- Don Shula
- Mike Krzyzewski
- Vince Lombardi
- Jose Mourinho
- Bill Walsh
- Pat Riley
- Dean Smith
- Christopher Sommer
- Freddie Roach
- Cus D'Amato

Classical & Jazz composers\ musicians

- Johann Sebastian Bach
- Amadeus Mozart
- Ludwig van Beethoven
- Frederic Chopin
- Igor Stravinsky
- Schoenberg
- Miles Davis
- Herbie Hancock
- Art Blakey
- Charlie Parker
- John Coltrane
- Chick Corea
- Keith Jarrett

Painters\ artists

- Picasso
- Dali
- Van Gogh
- Renoir
- Da Vinci
- Frida Kahlo
- Jackson Pollock
- Andy Warhol
- Monet
- Matisse

Psychologists

- Sigmund Freud
- BF Skinner
- Carl Jung
- Abraham Maslow
- Erikson
- Philip Zimbardo
- Erich Fromm
- Noam Chomsky
- Martin Seligman
- Viktor Frankl
- Steven Pinker
- Daniel Kahneman

Writers\ poets

- Mark Twain
- Ernest Hemingway
- J.K. Rowling
- Stephen King
- George Orwell
- William Shakespeare
- Roald Dahl
- Dr Seuss
- Franz Kafka
- Scott Fitzgerald
- Tolstoy
- Haruki Murakami
- TS Eliot
- J.D. Salinger
- Charles Bukowski
- Robert Frost

Designers

- Coco Chanel
- Tom Ford
- Alexander McQueen
- Karl Lagerfeld
- Marc Jacobs
- Dior

Explorers

- Sir Francis Drake
- Christopher Columbus
- Lewis and Clark
- Pizarro
- Vespucci
- Ferdinand Magellan
- Vasco Nunez de Balboa

Architects

- Frank Lloyd Wright
- Frank Gehry
- Santiago Calatrava
- Antoni Gaudi

- Buckminster Fuller (also inventor and designer)

Athletes

- Michael Jordan
- Magic Johnson
- Andre Agassi
- Pete Sampras
- Roger Federer
- Mike Tyson
- Muhammad Ali
- Arnold Schwarzenegger
- Usain Bolt
- Tiger Woods
- Lionel Messi
- Michael Phelps
- Pele
- Wayne Gretzky
- Bruce Lee
- Kareem Abdul Jabbar
- Nadia Comaneci
- Dan Gable
- Babe Ruth
- Jackie Robinson
- Deion Sanders
- Frank Shamrock

Scientists, Inventors

- Albert Einstein
- Isaac Newton
- Galileo
- Marie Curie
- Charles Darwin
- Stephen Hawking
- Nikola Tesla
- Thomas Edison
- Michio Kaku
- Copernicus
- Michael Faraday
- Leonardo Da Vinci
- Alexander Graham Bell
- Richard Feynman
- Neil degrasse Tyson
- Carl Sagan
- Benjamin Franklin

Historians

- Will Durant
- Thucydides
- Herodotus
- Niall Ferguson

Made in the USA
Middletown, DE
18 November 2018